Low FODMAP Cookbook for Beginners

From Distress to Digestive Bliss. Subdue IBS Symptoms with the Low FODMAP Diet.

30-days meal plan included

Dora Gibbons

EATS ADVICE

CHANGE YOUR DIET, CHANGE YOUR LIFE

Table of Contents

Author

Hi. My name is Dora, and I am an ordinary person passionate about healthy food and good nutrition. Unfortunately, I suffered from intestinal disorders that made my life difficult for a long time. I tried many diets and remedies, but without success, until I discovered the Low FODMAP diet.

From that moment, I became passionate about the world of nutrition. I started to attend seminars and discover new things about the Low FODMAP diet. Thanks to this diet, I have solved most of my intestinal problems and finally feel good.

I document myself daily by following forums and niche blogs on the Low FODMAP diet. Finally, I decided to write a book on this topic to help others who suffer from intestinal disorders.

In my book, I use a friendly tone and speak directly to the reader, as if talking to a long-time friend. I want to share my experience and help others solve their intestinal problems with the Low FODMAP diet, just as I did. If you are here reading this book, you are looking for a way to improve your health and relationship with food. I hope you will find many valuable insights in these pages. I wish you a happy reading!

Before you begin your reading, I invite you to download my prepared gift. Download it directly from eatsadvice.com, the sponsor of this book, by framing the QR code.

Finally, I would love to hear your honest opinion by leaving a review on Amazon.

Introduction

The low FODMAP diet is a temporary diet developed to help reduce gastrointestinal disorders such as irritable bowel syndrome (IBS) symptoms. The diet consists of limiting FODMAPs, short-chain carbohydrates that are difficult to digest and can cause bloating, gas, and other gastrointestinal symptoms.

The low FODMAP diet is divided into three phases: an elimination phase, a reintroduction phase, and a customization phase.

The elimination phase of the low FODMAP diet requires limiting the intake of high FODMAP foods for several weeks to reduce gastrointestinal symptoms. Foods high in FODMAPs include, for example, fructose (found in many fruits and vegetables, but also in some syrups), lactose (found in milk and dairy products), fructans (found in some vegetables, cereals, and gluten-containing foods), Galatians (found in some legumes and grains), and polyols (found in some artificial sweeteners and some fruits such as plums).

After the elimination phase, the reintroduction phase begins with the gradual introduction of FODMAPs one at a time to identify the specific foods causing gastrointestinal symptoms. During this phase, keeping a food diary and noting the symptoms after eating each food is essential. In this way, it can be determined which FODMAPs are responsible for gastrointestinal symptoms and which foods can be consumed without side effects.

Finally, in the customization phase, a long-term diet limits only the FODMAPs that cause symptoms. This personalized diet can be complex and requires effort to plan meals and prepare foods. Still, it can also lead to a significant reduction in gastrointestinal symptoms and improved quality of life. However, it is essential to note that the low FODMAP diet should not be considered a permanent solution for gastrointestinal disorders and should be adopted only under the supervision of a qualified health professional.

Before starting the low FODMAP diet, it is essential to consult a dietitian or physician to ensure that it is suitable for your needs and health condition. For example, the low FODMAP diet can benefit those with gastrointestinal disorders such as irritable bowel syndrome (IBS), but it is not suitable for everyone. For example, those with conditions such as celiac disease or lactose intolerance should discuss with a health professional before starting the low FODMAP diet.

Also, it is essential to know that the low FODMAP diet can be complex and require some effort to plan meals and prepare foods. In addition, the diet requires avoiding many foods that could be part of a balanced, healthy diet, so working with a health professional to develop a nutritionally complete eating plan is essential.

Despite the challenges, many have reported significantly reduced gastrointestinal symptoms and improved quality of life from the low FODMAP diet. However, suppose you choose to follow the diet. In that case, it is essential to do so under the supervision of a qualified health professional and make sure you are adequately informed about the foods you can and cannot eat. Also, it is important not to continue the low FODMAP diet long-term, as this can lead to nutritional deficiencies.

What is the Low FODMAP Diet

The low FODMAP diet is a temporary diet developed to help reduce gastrointestinal symptoms associated with disorders such as irritable bowel syndrome (IBS). The diet focuses on limiting the intake of short-chain carbohydrates known as FODMAP, which can be challenging to digest and cause gastrointestinal symptoms such as bloating, gas, diarrhea, and constipation.

FODMAP is an acronym for Fermentable Oligosaccharides, Disaccharides, Monosaccharides, and Polyols, or fermentable oligosaccharides, disaccharides, monosaccharides, and polyols. Fermentable oligosaccharides are chains of short sugars, such as fructose-oligosaccharide and galactose-oligosaccharide, found in foods such as garlic, onions, wheat, and some legumes. Disaccharides include lactose found in milk and dairy products. Monosaccharides include fructose, found in many fruits and sweeteners, and polyol has alcohol sugars such as xylitol, found in some chewing gum.

These carbohydrates are difficult to digest and can cause gastrointestinal symptoms such as bloating, gas, diarrhea, and constipation in some people, especially those with gastrointestinal disorders such as irritable bowel syndrome (IBS).

FODMAPs can be found in many common foods, such as fruits, vegetables, grains, legumes, and artificial sweeteners. Examples of foods high in FODMAPs include apples, oranges, asparagus, artichokes, mushrooms, garlic, onions, wheat, dairy products, and some sweeteners such as honey and agave.

The low FODMAP diet focuses on limiting the intake of these short-chain carbohydrates, which can be challenging to digest, to reduce gastrointestinal symptoms and improve the quality of life of people suffering from gastrointestinal disorders. During the elimination phase, high FODMAP foods are restricted for several weeks. Then, high FODMAP foods are gradually reintroduced in the reintroduction phase to identify those causing specific gastrointestinal symptoms. Finally, in the customization phase, a long-term diet limits only the FODMAPs that cause symptoms while trying to maintain a balanced and nutritious diet.

The low FODMAP diet was developed by the Monash University in Australia Department of Gastroenterology, led by Professor Peter Gibson and Dr. Susan Shepherd. Original research conducted by their team showed that FODMAPs may be a significant cause of gastrointestinal symptoms in some people suffering from disorders such as irritable bowel syndrome (IBS).

The low FODMAP diet has become increasingly popular in recent years. Many health professionals, including dietitians and nutritionists, use it to treat patients with IBS and other gastrointestinal disorders. In addition, the diet has been supported by numerous clinical research showing its effectiveness in reducing gastrointestinal symptoms in people with IBS and other conditions.

Many patients suffering from IBS or other gastrointestinal disorders have reported significantly reduced symptoms after following the low FODMAP diet. However, it is essential to note that the diet only works for some and may only be suitable for some patients. Therefore, discussing with a health professional whether the low FODMAP diet is ideal for your needs and health condition is necessary.

The low FODMAP diet is an important step forward in managing gastrointestinal symptoms. It has provided an effective treatment option for many people suffering from gastrointestinal disorders. However, it is essential to follow the diet under a qualified health professional's supervision and consult a physician or dietitian before following it long-term.

A 2014 study published in "Gastroenterology" showed that the low FODMAP diet can significantly reduce gastrointestinal symptoms in patients with IBS. The study involved 30 patients with IBS who followed the low FODMAP diet for 4 weeks. Compared with the control group, patients who followed the diet reported significantly reduced gastrointestinal symptoms such as bloating, abdominal pain, and diarrhea.

Another 2016 study published in "The Journal of Gastroenterology and Hepatology" compared the low FODMAP diet with a standard high-fiber diet in patients with IBS. The study involved 104 patients with IBS and showed that the low-FODMAP diet significantly reduced gastrointestinal symptoms more effectively than the high-fiber diet.

A 2017 systematic review published in "The Journal of Gastroenterology and Hepatology" evaluated the effects of a low FODMAP diet on gastrointestinal symptoms in patients with IBS. The review concluded that the low FODMAP diet can significantly reduce gastrointestinal symptoms in patients with IBS and may be an effective therapy.

However, it is essential to note that research on the low FODMAP diet is ongoing. As a result, there are still many open questions about its long-term efficacy and its effects on overall health. In addition, the low FODMAP diet should not be followed long-term without medical supervision because of the risk of nutritional deficiencies.

Symptoms Of Gastrointestinal Disorder

Gastrointestinal disorders can manifest with a wide range of symptoms, varying from person to person. However, some of the most common symptoms associated with irritable bowel syndrome (IBS) and other gastrointestinal disorders include:

- Abdominal pain
- Bloating
- Diarrhea
- Constipation
- Altered bowel habits.
- Nausea and vomiting
- Weight loss

Abdominal pain is a common symptom associated with many gastrointestinal disorders, such as irritable bowel syndrome (IBS), ulcerative colitis, Crohn's disease, and gastroenteritis. Abdominal pain can occur in different parts of the abdomen, ranging from mild to severe.

Common causes of abdominal pain include inflammation of the intestines, gas accumulation in the intestines, irritation of the intestines, and intestinal obstruction. In addition, in some cases, abdominal pain may be caused by non-gastrointestinal diseases, such as appendicitis, gallstones, or pancreatitis.

Abdominal pain may accompany other gastrointestinal symptoms, such as diarrhea, constipation, bloating, and nausea. Sometimes, abdominal pain may accompany non-gastrointestinal symptoms, such as fever, weight loss, or fatigue.

Abdominal bloating is a common symptom associated with many gastrointestinal disorders, such as irritable bowel syndrome (IBS), ulcerative colitis, and Crohn's disease. Abdominal bloating can make the abdomen feel bloated and tense and cause discomfort and heaviness.

Common causes of abdominal bloating include gas accumulation in the intestines, fluid retention, and inflammation of the intestines. Sometimes, abdominal bloating may be caused by non-gastrointestinal diseases, such as heart or kidney failure.

Abdominal bloating may accompany other gastrointestinal symptoms, such as abdominal pain, diarrhea, constipation, and nausea. Sometimes, abdominal bloating may also be accompanied by non-gastrointestinal symptoms, such as difficulty breathing, coughing, or loss of appetite.

Diarrhea is a common symptom associated with many gastrointestinal disorders, such as irritable bowel syndrome (IBS), ulcerative colitis, Crohn's disease, and gastrointestinal infection.

Diarrhea occurs when food passes too quickly through the intestines, causing frequent and liquid bowel evacuations. Diarrhea may accompany abdominal cramping, abdominal pain, bloating, and nausea. In some more severe cases, blood may also be in the stool.

Common causes of diarrhea include bacterial or viral infections, food intolerances, food allergies, nutrient malabsorption, bowel disorders, and side effects of some medications. In some cases, diarrhea may be a symptom of more severe disease, such as ulcerative colitis or Crohn's disease.

Treatment for diarrhea depends on the underlying cause. For example, treatments may include antibiotics or antiviral drugs in case of diarrhea caused by bacterial or viral infections. In case of diarrhea caused by food intolerances or allergies, treatment may include dietary changes, such as a low FODMAP diet. In cases of diarrhea caused by more severe gastrointestinal diseases, treatment may consist of immunosuppressive drugs, biological therapies, or surgery.

Constipation is a common symptom associated with many gastrointestinal disorders, such as irritable bowel syndrome (IBS), ulcerative colitis, Crohn's disease, and gastrointestinal insomnia.

Constipation occurs when the intestines do not empty regularly or when stools become too dry and hard, making bowel evacuation difficult. Common symptoms of constipation include difficulty in bowel evacuation, abdominal pain, bloating, and feeling full.

Common causes of constipation include a low-fiber diet, taking medications that cause constipation, a sedentary lifestyle, dehydration, nutrient malabsorption, thyroid disorders, and other medical disorders.

Treatment for constipation depends on the underlying cause. In cases of mild or occasional constipation, one can modify the diet, increase fiber, and water intake, and adopt a more active lifestyle with regular exercise. In cases of more severe constipation, laxative medications may be prescribed, or dietary therapies such as the low FODMAP diet may be recommended.

Altered bowel habits are a common symptom associated with many gastrointestinal disorders, such as irritable bowel syndrome (IBS), ulcerative colitis, Crohn's disease, and other gastrointestinal disorders.

People with IBS and other gastrointestinal disorders may notice a change in their bowel habits, such as an increase or decrease in the frequency of bowel evacuations or a change in stool consistency. These changes can be caused by several factors, such as inflammation of the intestines, gut dysbiosis, taking certain medications, stress, and diet.

Altered bowel habits may accompany other gastrointestinal symptoms, such as abdominal pain, bloating, diarrhea, or constipation. In some cases, changed bowel habits may be a symptom of more severe disease, such as ulcerative colitis or Crohn's disease.

Treatment for altered bowel habits depends on the underlying cause. In cases of IBS and other gastrointestinal disorders, treatment may include dietary therapies such as the low FODMAP diet, symptom control medications, stress management techniques, and psychological therapies. Treatment for more severe gastrointestinal disorders may include immunosuppressive drugs, biological medicines, or surgery.

Nausea and vomiting are common symptoms associated with many gastrointestinal disorders, such as irritable bowel syndrome (IBS), ulcerative colitis, Crohn's disease, and gastrointestinal infection.

Nausea occurs when there is a feeling of wanting to vomit, while vomiting is the forced release of stomach contents through the mouth. Nausea and vomiting can be caused by many conditions, such as inflammation of the intestines, accumulation of gas in the intestines, intestinal obstruction, irritation of the intestines, and the side effect of some medications.

Nausea and vomiting may accompany other gastrointestinal symptoms, such as abdominal pain, diarrhea, or constipation. In addition, in some cases, nausea and vomiting may be accompanied by non-gastrointestinal symptoms, such as fever, weight loss, or weakness.

Treatment for nausea and vomiting depends on the underlying cause. For example, in cases of nausea and vomiting caused by bacterial or viral infections, treatment may include antibiotics or antiviral drugs. In cases of nausea and vomiting caused by food intolerances or allergies, treatment may include dietary changes, such as a low FODMAP diet. In cases of nausea and vomiting caused by more severe gastrointestinal diseases, treatment may consist of immunosuppressive drugs, biological therapies, or surgery.

Involuntary weight loss is a common symptom associated with many medical conditions, including gastrointestinal disorders such as Crohn's disease, ulcerative colitis, celiac disease, and irritable bowel syndrome (IBS).

Unintentional weight loss occurs when you lose weight without trying, such as not dieting or exercising. In involuntary weight loss, you can lose weight quickly or gradually. The amount lost can vary depending on the underlying cause.

Common causes of unintentional weight loss include nutrient malabsorption, inflammation of the intestines, chronic diarrhea, nausea, vomiting, and decreased appetite. In some cases, involuntary weight loss may be a symptom of more severe diseases like cancer or HIV.

Treatment for involuntary weight loss depends on the underlying cause. For example, for unintentional weight loss caused by gastrointestinal disease, treatment may include dietary therapies, medications to control symptoms, or surgery in more severe cases. In case of accidental weight loss caused by other diseases, treatment will depend on the underlying condition.

Impact on overall health

The low FODMAP diet can significantly impact the overall health of people suffering from gastrointestinal disorders, such as irritable bowel syndrome (IBS), ulcerative colitis, Crohn's disease, and other gastrointestinal disorders.

In many cases, gastrointestinal symptoms can negatively affect people's quality of life, limiting their ability to participate in daily activities and causing anxiety, depression, and stress. The low FODMAP diet can help reduce gastrointestinal symptoms, improve quality of life, and reduce the emotional burden associated with the disease.

In addition, some studies have suggested that the low FODMAP diet may have other benefits on overall health, such as reducing intestinal inflammation, normalizing intestinal flora, and reducing the risk of heart disease and diabetes.

The low FODMAP diet can be complex and requires careful meal planning and evaluation of the foods that can be consumed. The diet also needs to reduce or eliminate foods that contain FODMAP, including some customarily considered healthy foods, such as fruits and vegetables.

In addition, the low FODMAP diet can reduce the intake of essential nutrients, such as fiber, which is critical for digestive health and overall well-being. Reduced fiber intake can lead to decreased intestinal motility and increased difficulty in stool elimination, causing or worsening constipation.

It is important to note that the low FODMAP diet should not be followed for an extended period, as it can lead to long-term nutritional deficiencies. In addition, the diet is not suitable for everyone. Therefore, it should be followed with the supervision of a health professional.

For these reasons, working with a dietitian or physician is essential to develop a personalized diet plan that meets individual nutritional needs and helps manage gastrointestinal symptoms. Sometimes, it may be necessary to supplement the low FODMAP diet with vitamin or mineral supplements to ensure adequate intake of essential nutrients.

Nutrition and supplementation

As mentioned earlier, the low FODMAP diet can reduce the intake of essential nutrients, such as fiber, critical for digestive health and overall well-being. Therefore, it is necessary for people on the low FODMAP diet to carefully evaluate their nutrient intake and supplement any deficiencies with foods and vitamin or mineral supplements.

For example, people on a low FODMAP diet may be at risk of vitamin D deficiency, which can be obtained mainly through sun exposure and intake of foods such as oily fish and fortified dairy products. In case of vitamin D deficiencies, it may be necessary to supplement the diet with vitamin or mineral supplements.

In addition, the low FODMAP diet may also lead to reduced fiber intake, which is critical for digestive health and the prevention of chronic diseases such as diabetes, cardiovascular disease, and colon cancer. Therefore, people on the low FODMAP diet must carefully supplement their diet with high-fiber foods such as fruits, vegetables, whole grains, legumes, and seeds.

Finally, the low FODMAP diet may lead to a reduced intake of probiotics, which are essential for healthy gut flora. People on the low FODMAP diet can supplement their diet with probiotic foods such as yogurt, kefir, fermented pickles, or probiotic supplements.

Probiotics are live microorganisms that occur naturally in the gastrointestinal tract and play an essential role in intestinal flora health. Studies have shown that probiotics can improve gastrointestinal symptoms, reduce intestinal inflammation, and promote good digestive health.

The low FODMAP diet may reduce probiotic intake because many foods high in probiotics, such as fermented dairy products, also contain FODMAPs. However, people on the low FODMAP diet can supplement their diet with probiotic foods such as yogurt, kefir, fermented pickles, or probiotic supplements.

Yogurt and kefir are familiar sources of probiotics. They are generally well tolerated by many people on the low FODMAP diet. It is important to choose yogurt and kefir without added sugar or artificial sweeteners, as these may contain FODMAP.

In addition, fermented pickles, such as gherkins, can be a good source of probiotics and are generally considered safe for people on the low FODMAP diet. However, it is essential to ensure that pickles do not contain other ingredients that may have FODMAPs, such as sugar or garlic.

Alternatively, people following the low FODMAP diet can supplement their diet with probiotic supplements. Probiotic supplements are available in different forms, including capsules, powders, and liquids. It is essential to choose high-quality probiotic supplements from reliable sources and follow the manufacturer's instructions.

Nutrition and supplementation are essential to ensure that people on the low FODMAP diet get all the nutrients they need for overall health and well-being. For this reason, it is necessary to work with a health professional to assess your diet and supplement any deficiencies with appropriate foods and supplements.

Social Life and Diet

Social life can be challenging for people on a low FODMAP diet, as it can be difficult to find suitable foods during social events, such as dinners or parties.

However, there are some strategies that people can use to deal with these challenges. For example, people can inform their friends and family members about their diet and the foods they need to avoid so that they can help prepare suitable meals during social events.

In addition, people can plan and look for restaurants or venues that offer low FODMAP menu options or are willing to prepare special meals upon request. Alternatively, people can bring their own meals and snacks to ensure they always have suitable food.

It is essential that people on the low FODMAP diet do not feel excluded from social life and can still attend social events and enjoy good food.

There are several options that people can consider enjoying delicious food, even while following the low FODMAP diet. For example, people can look for restaurants or places that offer low FODMAP menu options or are willing to prepare special meals upon request. Alternatively, people can bring suitable meals and snacks to ensure they always have the right food.

In addition, people can prepare suitable meals and snacks at home using low-FODMAP ingredients. Many delicious and healthy recipes are available online that use low FODMAP ingredients, such as soups, salads, and meat or fish preparations. In addition, people can experiment with different recipes to discover new flavors and combinations of ingredients.

Remembering that a low FODMAP diet should not prevent people from socializing and having fun with friends and family is also essential. People can still attend social events and enjoy delicious food, choosing only the options that fit their diet. People can enjoy an active social life and a healthy, balanced diet with careful planning and selecting suitable options.

His social life can be challenging for people on a low FODMAP diet. Still, some strategies can help overcome these challenges, such as informing friends and family about the diet, planning and looking for suitable menu options, or bringing convenient meals and snacks. It is important to remember that the diet should allow people to participate in social life and enjoy delicious food.

Support my Work

If you enjoyed the contents of this book and want to help me in a simple, accessible, and fast way, I'd love to hear your honest opinion. That way, other people looking for low FODMAP recipes will find my book and all my work. To do this, use the camera on your smartphone to scan the QR code or click on this link if you have the reader in the digital version.

Thank you, Katy.

Breakfast

1. Overnight Oats with Almond Milk and Blueberries

Preparation time: 5 minutes **Cooking Time:** 0 minutes **Servings:** 1 **Difficulty:** Easy

Ingredients:
- 1/2 cup gluten-free rolled oats.
- 1/2 cup unsweetened almond milk
- 1/2 cup fresh blueberries
- 1 tablespoon chia seeds
- 1 tablespoon maple syrup
- 1/2 teaspoon vanilla extract

Instructions:
1. Mix the rolled oats, almond milk, chia seeds, maple syrup, and vanilla extract until well combined in a jar or container with a lid.
2. Add the blueberries to the mixture and stir gently.
3. Cover the jar or container with a lid and refrigerate overnight or for at least 4 hours.
4. When ready to serve, stir the mixture well and add a little extra almond milk if desired for a creamier consistency.
5. If desired, top with additional blueberries or other low-FODMAP fruit and enjoy!

Nutritional Values: Calories: 280kcal Fat: 7g Carbohydrates: 47g Protein: 8g Fiber: 11g Sugar: 14g Sodium: 90mg

2. Spinach, Banana, And Almond Milk Smoothie

Preparation time: 5 minutes **Cooking Time:** 0 minutes **Servings:** 1 **Difficulty:** Easy

Ingredients:
- 1 ripe banana peeled and frozen.
- 1 cup fresh spinach leaves
- 1/2 cup unsweetened almond milk
- 1 tablespoon chia seeds
- 1/2 teaspoon vanilla extract

Instructions:
1. Add the frozen banana, spinach leaves, almond milk, chia seeds, and vanilla extract in a blender.
2. Blend on high speed until smooth and creamy.
3. If the smoothie is too thick, add extra almond milk until desired consistency is reached.
4. Pour into a glass and enjoy!

Nutritional Values: Calories: 250kcal Fat: 7g Carbohydrates: 44g Protein: 6g Fiber: 10g Sugar: 18g Sodium: 160mg

3. Pancakes With Maple Syrup and Strawberries

Preparation time: 10 minutes **Cooking Time:** 15 minutes **Servings:** 4-6 pancakes **Difficulty:** Easy

Ingredients:
- 1 cup gluten-free all-purpose flour
- 1 tablespoon sugar
- 1 teaspoon baking powder
- 1/2 teaspoon baking soda

- 1/4 teaspoon salt
- 1 cup lactose-free milk
- 1 large egg
- 1 tablespoon vegetable oil
- 1 teaspoon vanilla extract
- Maple syrup for serving.
- Fresh strawberries, sliced, for serving.

Instructions:

1. Whisk together the gluten-free all-purpose flour, sugar, baking powder, baking soda, and salt in a large bowl.
2. Whisk the lactose-free milk, egg, vegetable oil, and vanilla extract in a separate bowl.
3. Pour the wet ingredients into the dry ingredients and stir until combined. Stay undermixed.
4. Heat a nonstick skillet over medium heat. Using a 1/4 cup measure, pour the pancake batter into the skillet.
5. Cook the pancakes for 2-3 minutes until bubbles form on the surface and the edges start to set.
6. Flip the pancakes and cook for 1-2 minutes, until golden brown.
7. Repeat with the remaining batter, adjusting the heat as necessary.
8. Serve the pancakes warm with maple syrup and fresh strawberries.

Nutritional Values: Calories: 140kcal Fat: 4g Carbohydrates: 23g Protein: 3g Fiber: 1g Sugar: 6g Sodium: 230mg

4. Scrambled Eggs with Spinach and Feta Cheese

Preparation time: 10 minutes **Cooking Time:** 10 minutes **Servings:** 2 **Difficulty:** Easy
Ingredients:

- 4 large eggs
- 2 tablespoons lactose-free milk
- 1 cup fresh spinach leaves, chopped.
- 1/4 cup crumbled feta cheese
- Salt and pepper, to taste
- 1 tablespoon olive oil

Instructions:

1. Whisk the eggs and lactose-free milk in a bowl until well combined.
2. Heat the olive oil in a nonstick skillet over medium heat.
3. Add the chopped spinach to the skillet and sauté for 1-2 minutes, until wilted.
4. Pour the egg mixture into the skillet and cook, stirring occasionally, for 2-3 minutes, until the eggs are set but still moist.
5. Add the crumbled feta cheese to the skillet and stir gently to combine.
6. Season with salt and pepper to taste.
7. Serve hot and enjoy!

Nutritional Values: Calories: 220kcal Fat: 18g Carbohydrates: 2g Protein: 13g Fiber: 1g Sugar: 1g Sodium: 310mg

5. Greek Yogurt with Granola and Mixed Berries

Preparation time: 5 minutes **Cooking Time:** 0 minutes **Servings:** 1 **Difficulty:** Easy
Ingredients:

- 1/2 cup low FODMAP granola
- 1/2 cup lactose-free Greek yogurt
- 1/2 cup mixed berries (e.g., blueberries, strawberries, raspberries)

Instructions:

1. Layer the low-FODMAP granola, lactose-free Greek yogurt, and mixed berries in a bowl.

2. Repeat the layering until all the ingredients are used up.
3. Serve immediately and enjoy!

Nutritional Values: Calories: 320kcal Fat: 9g Carbohydrates: 50g Protein: 14g Fiber: 7g Sugar: 19g Sodium: 120mg

6. Chia Seed Pudding with Coconut Milk and Kiwi Fruit

Preparation time: 5 minutes **Cooking Time:** 0 minutes Chilling time: 3 hours **Servings:** 2 **Difficulty:** Easy
Ingredients:
- 1/4 cup chia seeds
- 1 cup coconut milk
- 2 tablespoons maple syrup
- 1 teaspoon vanilla extract
- 1 kiwi fruit, sliced.

Instructions:
1. Mix the chia seeds, coconut milk, maple syrup, and vanilla extract until well combined.
2. Let the mixture sit for 5-10 minutes, then whisk again to prevent clumping.
3. Cover the bowl with plastic wrap and refrigerate for at least 3 hours or overnight.
4. When ready to serve, divide the chia seed pudding between two bowls.
5. Top with sliced kiwi fruit and serve chilled.

Nutritional Values: Calories: 280kcal Fat: 18g Carbohydrates: 22g Protein: 5g Fiber: 11g Sugar: 7g
Sodium: 30mg

7. Breakfast Burrito with Scrambled Eggs, Turkey Bacon, And Spinach

Preparation time: 10 minutes **Cooking Time:** 15 minutes **Servings:** 2 **Difficulty:** Easy
Ingredients:
- 4 eggs
- 4 slices of turkey bacon, chopped.
- 1 cup spinach leaves
- 1/2 teaspoon garlic powder
- Salt and pepper to taste
- 2 low FODMAP tortillas

Instructions:
1. In a nonstick skillet, cook the chopped turkey bacon over medium heat until crispy. Remove from the skillet and set aside.
2. Add the spinach and cook until wilted in the same skillet.
3. In a bowl, beat the eggs with garlic powder, salt, and pepper.
4. Add the beaten eggs to the skillet with the wilted spinach and cook, stirring occasionally, until the eggs are scrambled and fully cooked.
5. Warm the tortillas in the microwave for 15-20 seconds.
6. Divide the scrambled eggs and turkey bacon between the tortillas, roll them up, and serve immediately.

Nutritional Values: Calories: 320kcal Fat: 14g Carbohydrates: 21g Protein: 26g Fiber: 3g Sugar: 1g Sodium: 720mg

8. Quinoa And Egg Breakfast Bowl with Sautéed Kale and Cherry Tomatoes

Preparation time: 10 minutes **Cooking Time:** 20 minutes **Servings:** 2 **Difficulty:** Easy
Ingredients:

- 1/2 cup quinoa
- 1 cup water
- 2 eggs
- 2 cups kale, chopped.
- 1 cup cherry tomatoes, halved.
- 1/2 teaspoon garlic powder
- Salt and pepper to taste
- 1 tablespoon olive oil

Instructions:

1. Rinse the quinoa and put it in a pot with 1 cup of water. Bring to a boil, then reduce the heat and let simmer for 15-20 minutes until the water is absorbed and the quinoa is cooked.
2. Heat the olive oil over medium heat in a nonstick skillet.
3. Add the chopped kale and cook until wilted, stirring occasionally.
4. Add the cherry tomatoes, garlic powder, salt, and pepper, and cook for 2-3 more minutes until the tomatoes are soft.
5. In another nonstick skillet, fry the eggs to your desired doneness over medium heat.
6. To assemble the bowls, divide the cooked quinoa between two bowls, add the sautéed kale and cherry tomatoes, and top with the fried eggs.
7. Serve immediately.

Nutritional Values: Calories: 290kcal Fat: 12g Carbohydrates: 30g Protein: 14g Fiber: 6g Sugar: 4g Sodium: 80mg

9. Breakfast Sausage Patties with Roasted Sweet Potatoes

Preparation time: 10 minutes **Cooking Time:** 30 minutes **Servings:** 4 **Difficulty:** Easy
Ingredients:

- 1 lb. ground pork
- 1 tablespoon fresh sage, chopped.
- 1/2 teaspoon dried thyme
- 1/2 teaspoon garlic powder
- 1/2 teaspoon salt
- 1/4 teaspoon black pepper
- 2 medium sweet potatoes peeled and diced.
- 1 tablespoon olive oil

Instructions:

1. Preheat the oven to 400°F (200°C) and line a baking sheet with parchment paper.
2. Combine the ground pork, sage, thyme, garlic powder, salt, and pepper in a mixing bowl. Mix well to combine.
3. Form the pork mixture into small patties, about 2-3 inches in diameter.
4. Heat a nonstick skillet over medium heat and cook the sausage patties for 2-3 minutes per side until browned and cooked.
5. Toss the diced sweet potatoes with olive oil and spread them on the prepared baking sheet.
6. Roast the sweet potatoes in the oven for 20-25 minutes until tender and lightly browned.
7. Serve the sausage patties with the roasted sweet potatoes on the side.

Nutritional Values: Calories: 365kcal Fat: 26g Carbohydrates: 11g Protein: 20g Fiber: 2g Sugar: 4g Sodium: 426mg

10. Tofu Scramble with Bell Peppers and Mushrooms

Preparation time: 10 minutes **Cooking Time:** 15 minutes **Servings:** 2-3 **Difficulty:** Easy
Ingredients:

- 1 block (14 oz) firm tofu, drained and pressed.
- 1/2 red bell pepper, diced.
- 1/2 green bell pepper, diced.
- 1 cup sliced mushrooms.
- 1/2 tsp ground turmeric
- 1/2 tsp smoked paprika.
- 1/2 tsp garlic powder
- 1/2 tsp onion powder
- Salt and pepper, to taste
- 2 tbsp olive oil
- Fresh parsley, chopped (for garnish)

Instructions:

1. Heat the olive oil over medium heat in a large skillet.
2. Add the diced bell peppers and mushrooms to the skillet and sauté for about 5-7 minutes until softening.
3. Crumble the tofu into the skillet and add the turmeric, smoked paprika, garlic powder, onion powder, salt, and pepper.
4. Cook the tofu scramble, stirring frequently, until heated through and lightly browned, about 5-7 minutes.
5. Serve hot, garnished with chopped fresh parsley.

Nutritional Values: Calories: 202 kcal Fat: 16g Carbohydrates: 7g Fiber: 2g Protein: 11g Sodium: 195mg Sugar: 2g

11. Buckwheat Porridge with Banana and Cinnamon

Preparation time: 5 minutes **Cooking Time:** 20 minutes **Servings:** 2 **Difficulty:** Easy
Ingredients:

- 1 cup of buckwheat groats
- 2 cups of water
- 1 ripe banana, mashed.
- 1 tsp cinnamon
- 1/4 tsp salt
- 1/2 cup of almond milk
- 2 tbsp maple syrup (optional)
- 1/4 cup of chopped walnuts (optional)

Instructions:

1. Rinse the buckwheat groats under cold water and drain well.
2. In a medium-sized saucepan, bring the water to a boil.
3. Combine the buckwheat groats, mashed banana, cinnamon, and salt in the saucepan.
4. Keep the heat low and cover the saucepan with a lid.
5. Cook the porridge for 15-20 minutes or until the buckwheat is tender and the water has been absorbed.
6. Stir in the almond milk and maple syrup (if using) until well combined.
7. Serve the porridge hot, topped with chopped walnuts (if using).

Nutritional Values: Calories: 291 kcal Protein: 8 g Fat: 6 g Carbohydrates: 55 g Fiber: 8 g Sugar: 11 g Sodium: 303 mg Potassium: 520 mg Calcium: 100 mg Iron: 2.9 mg

12. Breakfast Frittata with Spinach and Cheddar Cheese

Preparation time: 10 minutes **Cooking Time:** 25 minutes **Servings:** 4 **Difficulty:** Easy
Ingredients:

- 8 large eggs
- 1/4 cup lactose-free milk
- 2 tablespoons garlic-infused oil
- 2 cups baby spinach
- 1/2 cup shredded cheddar cheese
- Salt and pepper to taste

Instructions:

1. Preheat the oven to 375°F (190°C).
2. Whisk the eggs and lactose-free milk in a mixing bowl.
3. Heat the garlic-infused oil in a 10-inch oven-safe skillet over medium heat.
4. Add the baby spinach to the skillet and sauté until wilted.
5. Pour the egg mixture over the spinach and cook until the edges begin to set.
6. Sprinkle the shredded cheddar cheese over the eggs.
7. Transfer the skillet to the preheated oven and bake for 15-20 minutes or until the frittata is fully set.
8. Remove from the oven and let it cool for a few minutes.
9. Use a spatula to loosen the frittata from the skillet and transfer it to a serving plate.
10. Slice the frittata into wedges and serve.

Nutritional Values: Calories: 235 kcal Fat: 18g Carbohydrates: 2g Protein: 16g Fiber: 1g

13. Waffles With Raspberry Jam

Preparation time: 10 minutes **Cooking Time:** 15 minutes **Servings:** 4 **Difficulty:** Easy
Ingredients:

- 1 1/2 cups gluten-free all-purpose flour
- 1/4 cup cornstarch
- 1 tablespoon baking powder
- 1/4 teaspoon salt
- 1 tablespoon sugar
- 2 eggs, separated.
- 1 1/2 cups almond milk
- 1/4 cup coconut oil, melted.
- 1 teaspoon vanilla extract
- Cooking spray
- Low FODMAP raspberry jam

Instructions:

1. Preheat the waffle iron according to the manufacturer's instructions.
2. Whisk together the gluten-free flour, cornstarch, baking powder, salt, and sugar in a large mixing bowl.
3. In a separate mixing bowl, beat the egg whites until stiff peaks form.
4. Whisk the egg yolks, almond milk, melted coconut oil, and vanilla extract in another mixing bowl.
5. Add the egg yolk mixture to the dry ingredients and mix until well combined.
6. Gently fold in the beaten egg whites.
7. Spray the preheated waffle iron with cooking spray.
8. Pour batter onto the waffle iron and cook until golden brown.
9. Serve with low-FODMAP raspberry jam.

Nutritional Values: Calories: 402 kcal Fat: 21g Carbohydrates: 47g Fiber: 2g Protein: 8g

14. Breakfast Wrap with Scrambled Eggs, Turkey Bacon, And Avocado

Preparation time: 10 minutes **Cooking Time:** 15 minutes **Servings:** 2 **Difficulty:** Easy

Ingredients:

- 4 large eggs
- 4 slices of turkey bacon, chopped.
- 1/2 avocado, sliced.
- 2 gluten-free low FODMAP tortillas
- Salt and pepper, to taste
- Olive oil for cooking

Instructions:

1. Heat a nonstick skillet over medium heat and add the chopped turkey bacon. Cook for 5-7 minutes or until crispy, then remove from the pan and set aside.
2. Whisk together the eggs with a pinch of salt and pepper in a bowl.
3. Return the skillet to medium heat and add a drizzle of olive oil. Pour in the eggs and scramble until cooked through about 2-3 minutes.
4. Warm the tortillas in the microwave or in a dry skillet.
5. Divide the scrambled eggs, turkey bacon, and sliced avocado between the tortillas.
6. Roll up the tortillas tightly, tucking in the ends to create a burrito.
7. Slice in half and serve immediately.

Nutritional Values: Calories: 355 kcal Fat: 24g Carbohydrates: 18g Fiber: 6g Protein: 18g

15. Breakfast Muffins with Blueberries and Almond Flour

Preparation time: 15 minutes **Cooking Time:** 20 minutes **Servings:** 12 muffins **Difficulty:** Easy

Ingredients:

- 2 cups almond flour
- 1/2 cup oat flour
- 1 tsp baking powder
- 1/2 tsp baking soda
- 1/2 tsp salt
- 2 eggs
- 1/4 cup maple syrup
- 1/4 cup almond milk
- 1/4 cup coconut oil, melted.
- 1 tsp vanilla extract
- 1 cup fresh blueberries

Instructions:

1. Preheat the oven to 350°F (175°C) and line a muffin tin with paper liners.
2. Whisk together the almond flour, oat flour, baking powder, baking soda, and salt in a large bowl.
3. Whisk together the eggs, maple syrup, almond milk, melted coconut oil, and vanilla extract in a separate bowl.
4. Pour the wet ingredients into the dry ingredients and stir until combined.
5. Gently fold in the blueberries.
6. Divide the batter evenly between the prepared muffin cups.
7. Bake for 18-20 minutes, or until a toothpick inserted in the center of a muffin comes out clean.
8. Allow the muffins to cool in the tin for 5 minutes before transferring them to a wire rack to cool completely.

Nutritional Values: Calories: 202 kcal Protein: 6 g Fat: 17 g Saturated Fat: 4 g Carbohydrates: 10 g Fiber: 3 g Sugar: 5 g Sodium: 182 mg

16. Poached Eggs with Toast and Butter

Preparation time: 5 minutes **Cooking Time:** 5-7 minutes **Servings:** 1 **Difficulty:** Easy

Ingredients:

- 1-2 large eggs
- 1 slice of gluten-free, low-FODMAP bread
- 1-2 teaspoons of butter (lactose-free or vegan alternative)
- Salt and pepper to taste
- Water

Instructions:

1. Fill a medium-sized saucepan with water and bring it to a gentle simmer over medium heat.
2. Crack the eggs into separate small bowls.
3. Once the water is simmering, use a spoon to create a whirlpool in the center of the saucepan.
4. Gently pour one egg into the center of the whirlpool and let it cook for 3-4 minutes for a soft yolk or 5-7 minutes for a firm yolk.
5. Use a slotted spoon to carefully remove the poached egg from the water and set it aside.
6. Repeat the process with the second egg.
7. Toast the gluten-free low FODMAP bread and spread butter on it.
8. Place the poached eggs on the toast, and sprinkle with salt and pepper to taste.
9. Serve hot and enjoy!

Nutritional Values: Calories: 270kcal Fat: 17g Carbohydrates: 17g Protein: 12g Fiber: 2g

17. Breakfast Quesadilla with Scrambled Eggs, Cheese, And Salsa

Preparation time: 10 minutes **Cooking Time:** 10 minutes **Servings:** 2 **Difficulty:** Easy

Ingredients:

- 4 gluten-free low FODMAP tortillas
- 4 eggs
- 1/2 cup of shredded cheddar cheese
- 1/4 cup of low FODMAP salsa
- Salt and pepper to taste
- Olive oil or cooking spray.

Instructions:

1. Crack the eggs into a bowl and beat them until well-mixed. Add salt and pepper to taste.
2. Heat a nonstick skillet over medium heat and lightly coat it with olive oil or cooking spray.
3. Pour the eggs into the skillet and cook, stirring occasionally, until they are scrambled and cooked.
4. Remove the eggs from the skillet and set them aside.
5. Clean the skillet and place it back on the heat.
6. Place one tortilla in the skillet and sprinkle 1/4 cup of cheese.
7. Add half of the scrambled eggs and 2 tablespoons of salsa on top of the cheese.
8. Top with another tortilla and cook for 1-2 minutes, until the cheese is melted, and the tortilla is crispy.
9. Flip the quesadilla and cook for another

1-2 minutes, until the other side is crispy, and the cheese is melted.

10. Repeat with the remaining ingredients to make the second quesadilla.
11. Cut the quesadillas into wedges and serve.

Nutritional Values: Calories: 433 kcal Fat: 23 g Carbohydrates: 32 g Fiber: 3 g Protein: 23 g

18. Breakfast Bowl with Roasted Sweet Potato, Spinach, And Poached Egg

Preparation time: 10 minutes **Cooking Time:** 30 minutes **Servings:** 2 **Difficulty:** Easy
Ingredients:

- 1 medium sweet potato peeled and diced.
- 1 tablespoon olive oil
- Salt and pepper, to taste
- 2 cups spinach
- 4 large eggs
- 2 teaspoons white vinegar

Instructions:

1. Preheat the oven to 400°F (200°C).
2. Toss the diced sweet potato with olive oil, salt, and pepper on a baking sheet. Roast for 25-30 minutes or until tender and lightly browned.
3. In a large skillet over medium heat, sauté the spinach until wilted, about 2-3 minutes.
4. Bring a pot of water to a gentle simmer and add the white vinegar. Crack each egg into a small bowl, then carefully drop it into the water. Cook for 3-4 minutes or until the whites are set, but the yolks are still runny.
5. Divide the roasted sweet potato and sautéed spinach between two bowls.

Top each with two poached eggs. Season with salt and pepper to taste.
Nutritional Values: Calories: 225 Fat: 13g Carbohydrates: 19g Fiber: 4g Protein: 11g

19. Breakfast Bagel with Cream Cheese and Smoked Salmon

Cooking Time: 0 minutes **Servings:** 1 **Difficulty:** Easy
Ingredients:

- 1 gluten-free low FODMAP bagel
- 2 tbsp lactose-free cream cheese
- 2 oz smoked salmon
- 1 tbsp chopped chives
- Salt and pepper to taste

Instructions:

1. Slice the bagel in half and toast if desired.
2. Spread the lactose-free cream cheese on both halves of the bagel.
3. Top half the bagel with the smoked salmon and sprinkle with chopped chives.
4. Season with salt and pepper to taste.
5. Close the bagel with the other half and serve.

Nutritional Values: Calories: 345 kcal Fat: 15 g Carbohydrates: 28 g Fiber: 4 g Protein: 24 g Sodium: 881 mg

20. Sandwich With Turkey Sausage, Egg, And Cheddar Cheese

Preparation time: 10 minutes **Cooking Time:** 15 minutes **Servings:** 2 **Difficulty:** Easy
Ingredients:

- 2 gluten-free low FODMAP English muffins

- 4 turkey breakfast sausage patties
- 2 eggs
- 2 slices cheddar cheese
- Salt and pepper to taste
- 1 tablespoon olive oil

Instructions:

1. Preheat oven to 350°F.
2. Cook turkey sausage patties in a pan over medium heat until browned on both sides, about 5-7 minutes. Set aside.
3. Crack eggs into a bowl, season with salt and pepper, and whisk together.
4. Heat olive oil in a nonstick pan over medium heat. Pour in the egg mixture and scramble until cooked through about 3-5 minutes. Set aside.
5. Cut English muffins in half and toast in the oven for 5-7 minutes.
6. Assemble the sandwich: place 2 turkey sausage patties, scrambled eggs, and a slice of cheddar cheese on the bottom half of each English muffin. Top with the other half of the muffin.
7. Serve hot and enjoy!

Nutritional Values: Calories: 530 kcal Fat: 33 g Carbohydrates: 26 g Protein: 30 g Fiber: 3 g Sugar: 1 g Sodium: 620 mg

21. Cinnamon Rolls with Cream Cheese Frosting

Preparation time: 20 minutes **Cooking Time:** 25-30 minutes **Servings:** 8-10 rolls **Difficulty:** Medium

Ingredients:

For the dough:
- 1 cup gluten-free all-purpose flour
- 1 cup buckwheat flour
- 1/4 cup white sugar
- 1 tablespoon baking powder
- 1/2 teaspoon baking soda
- 1/2 teaspoon salt
- 1/2 cup unsweetened almond milk
- 1/4 cup melted butter.
- 1 egg
- 1 teaspoon vanilla extract

For the filling:
- 1/4 cup unsalted butter, softened.
- 1/4 cup brown sugar
- 1 tablespoon ground cinnamon

For the frosting:
- 4 oz cream cheese, softened.
- 1/4 cup unsalted butter, softened.
- 1 1/2 cups powdered sugar.
- 1/2 teaspoon vanilla extract

Instructions:

1. Preheat oven to 375°F (190°C). Line a 9-inch cake pan with parchment paper.
2. Whisk together the gluten-free all-purpose flour, buckwheat flour, sugar, baking powder, baking soda, and salt in a large mixing bowl.
3. Whisk together the almond milk, melted butter, egg, and vanilla extract in a separate bowl.
4. Add the wet and dry ingredients and stir until well combined.
5. Roll out the dough into a rectangle about 1/4 inch thick on a lightly floured surface.
6. Spread the softened butter evenly over the dough. Sprinkle the brown sugar and cinnamon over the butter.
7. Roll the dough up tightly from the long edge, using a sharp knife to cut into 1 1/2-inch rolls.
8. Place the rolls in the prepared cake pan, cut side up. Bake for 25-30 minutes or until golden brown.

9. While the rolls are baking, prepare the frosting. In a medium mixing bowl, beat the cream cheese and butter until smooth.
10. Add the powdered sugar and vanilla extract and continue to beat until the frosting is smooth and creamy.
11. Once the rolls are finished baking, let them cool for 5 minutes. Then, spread the cream cheese frosting evenly over the rolls.
12. Serve and enjoy!

Nutritional Values: Calories: 330 kcal Fat: 17 g Carbohydrates: 40 g Fiber: 3 g Protein: 5 g Sodium: 330 mg

22. Breakfast Pizza with Tomato Sauce, Mozzarella Cheese, And Turkey Sausage

Preparation time: 10 minutes **Cooking Time:** 20 minutes **Servings:** 2-4 **Difficulty:** Easy
Ingredients:
- 1 gluten-free low FODMAP pizza crust
- 1/2 cup low FODMAP tomato sauce
- 1/2 cup shredded mozzarella cheese
- 4 oz cooked low FODMAP turkey sausage, sliced.
- 2 large eggs
- Salt and pepper, to taste

Instructions:
1. Preheat the oven to 425°F (218°C).
2. Place the pizza crust on a baking sheet.
3. Spread the tomato sauce on the pizza crust, leaving a 1/2-inch border around the edges.
4. Sprinkle the shredded mozzarella cheese over the tomato sauce.
5. Add the sliced turkey sausage on top of the cheese.
6. Crack the eggs on the pizza, spacing them out evenly.
7. Season the pizza with salt and pepper.
8. Bake for 15-20 minutes or until the crust is golden brown and the eggs are set.
9. Slice and serve hot.

Nutritional Values: Calories: 392 kcal Fat: 22 g Carbohydrates: 28 g Fiber: 2 g Protein: 21 g Sodium: 773 mg Sugar: 3 g

23. Breakfast Quiche with Bacon and Cheddar Cheese

Preparation time: 15 minutes **Cooking Time:** 40 minutes **Servings:** 6 **Difficulty:** Easy
Ingredients:
- 1 gluten-free pie crust
- 6 slices of bacon cooked and chopped.
- 1 cup shredded cheddar cheese
- 4 large eggs
- 1 cup lactose-free milk
- 1/4 tsp salt
- 1/4 tsp black pepper

Instructions:
1. Preheat the oven to 350°F (175°C).
2. Whisk the eggs, lactose-free milk, salt, and black pepper in a mixing bowl.
3. Layer the chopped bacon and shredded cheddar cheese in the gluten-free pie crust.
4. Pour the egg mixture over the bacon and cheese.
5. Bake for 35-40 minutes or until the quiche is set.
6. Let the quiche cool for 10 minutes before slicing and serving.

Nutritional Values: Calories: 328 kcal Fat: 25g Carbohydrates: 15g Fiber: 0g Protein: 12g

24. Breakfast Omelet with Spinach and Cheddar Cheese

Preparation time: 5 minutes **Cooking Time:** 10 minutes **Servings:** 1 **Difficulty:** Easy

Ingredients:

- 2 large eggs
- 1/4 cup fresh spinach, chopped.
- 1/4 cup cheddar cheese, shredded.
- 1 tablespoon unsalted butter
- Salt and pepper, to taste

Instructions:

1. Whisk together the eggs and salt and pepper to taste in a small bowl.
2. Melt the butter in a nonstick skillet over medium heat.
3. Add the chopped spinach to the skillet and sauté until wilted, about 1-2 minutes.
4. Pour the eggs into the skillet and cook for 2-3 minutes or until the edges start to set.
5. Using a spatula, lift the edges of the omelet and let the uncooked eggs flow underneath.
6. When the omelet is mostly set but still slightly runny on top, sprinkle the shredded cheddar cheese over one-half of the omelet.
7. Use the spatula to fold the other half of the omelet over the cheese and cook for an additional 1-2 minutes until the cheese is melted and the eggs are cooked through.
8. Slide the omelet onto a plate and serve immediately.

Nutritional Values: Calories: 327 kcal Protein: 22 g Fat: 25 g Carbohydrates: 2 g Fiber: 0.5 g Sugar: 1 g Sodium: 444 mg

25. Breakfast Scones with Raspberry Jam

Preparation time: 15 minutes **Cooking Time:** 20-25 minutes **Servings:** 8 scones **Difficulty:** Easy

Ingredients:

- 2 cups gluten-free all-purpose flour
- 1/4 cup granulated sugar
- 2 tsp baking powder
- 1/2 tsp baking soda
- 1/2 tsp salt
- 6 tbsp unsalted butter, chilled and cut into small pieces.
- 1/2 cup lactose-free milk
- 2 large eggs
- 1 tsp vanilla extract
- 1/2 cup fresh or frozen raspberries
- 1/4 cup raspberry jam

Instructions:

1. Preheat the oven to 400°F (200°C). Line a baking sheet with parchment paper.
2. Whisk together the flour, sugar, baking powder, baking soda, and salt in a large bowl.
3. Add the chilled butter and use a pastry cutter or your hands to work the butter into the flour mixture until it resembles coarse sand.
4. Whisk together the milk, eggs, and vanilla extract in a separate bowl. Add the wet mixture to the dry mix and stir until just combined.
5. Fold in the raspberries.
6. Turn the dough onto a floured surface and shape it into a circle about 1 inch (2.5 cm) thick.
7. Transfer the circle into 8 wedges to the prepared baking sheet.

8. Bake for 20-25 minutes or until golden brown and cooked through.
9. Let the scones cool for 5 minutes before brushing them with raspberry jam.

Nutritional Values: Calories: 264 Fat: 12g Carbohydrates: 35g Fiber: 2g Protein: 4g Sodium: 315mg Potassium: 100mg Sugar: 10g

26. Breakfast Skillet with Turkey Sausage, Spinach, And Sweet Potato

Preparation time: 10 minutes **Cooking Time:** 25 minutes **Servings:** 4 **Difficulty:** Easy

Ingredients:

- 1 large, sweet potato, peeled and diced.
- 2 tablespoons olive oil
- 1/2-pound ground turkey sausage
- 2 cups fresh spinach
- 1/2 teaspoon paprika
- Salt and black pepper, to taste
- 4 eggs

Instructions:

1. Preheat oven to 375°F (190°C).
2. Heat the olive oil over medium heat in a large skillet. Add the diced sweet potato and cook for 10-12 minutes or until tender.
3. Add the ground turkey sausage to the skillet and cook for 5-7 minutes or until browned.
4. Add the fresh spinach to the skillet and cook until wilted.
5. Season the skillet with paprika, salt, and black pepper.
6. Crack the eggs over the skillet, ensuring they are spaced evenly apart.
7. Transfer the skillet to the preheated oven and bake for 8-10 minutes or until the eggs are set.
8. Serve hot and enjoy!

Nutritional Values: Calories: 311kcal Fat: 20g Carbohydrates: 14g Protein: 18g Fiber: 2g Sugar: 3g Sodium: 351mg

27. Breakfast Salad with Mixed Greens

Preparation time: 10 minutes **Cooking Time:** 10 minutes (for hard-boiled egg) **Servings:** 1 **Difficulty:** Easy

Ingredients:

- 2 cups mixed greens
- 1/2 cup cherry tomatoes, halved.
- 1 hard-boiled egg, sliced.
- 1 tbsp olive oil
- 1 tbsp balsamic vinegar
- Salt and pepper, to taste

Instructions:

1. Wash and dry the mixed greens and place them in a bowl.
2. Add the cherry tomatoes and sliced hard-boiled egg on top of the greens.
3. Whisk together the olive oil and balsamic vinegar in a small bowl to make the dressing.
4. Drizzle the dressing over the salad and sprinkle with salt and pepper.
5. Toss the salad gently to combine all the ingredients.
6. Serve immediately and enjoy!

Nutritional Values: Calories: 255kcal Carbohydrates: 8g Protein: 12g Fat: 20g Saturated Fat: 4g Cholesterol: 186mg Sodium: 130mg Potassium: 410mg Fiber: 2g Sugar: 4g Vitamin A: 74% DV Vitamin C: 38% DV Calcium: 8% DV Iron: 12% DV

28. Breakfast Crepes with Mixed

Berries and Coconut Whipped Cream

Preparation time: 10 minutes **Cooking Time:** 20 minutes **Servings:** 4 **Difficulty:** Medium
Ingredients:
- 1 cup gluten-free flour
- 1 tablespoon sugar
- 1/4 teaspoon salt
- 1 1/4 cup lactose-free milk
- 2 eggs
- 2 tablespoons vegetable oil
- 1 cup mixed berries (strawberries, blueberries, raspberries)
- 1 can full-fat coconut milk chilled overnight.
- 1 tablespoon maple syrup
- 1 teaspoon vanilla extract

Instructions:
1. Whisk together the gluten-free flour, sugar, and salt in a mixing bowl.
2. Add lactose-free milk, eggs, and vegetable oil, and whisk until the batter is smooth.
3. Heat a nonstick pan over medium heat and pour 1/4 cup of batter into the pan.
4. Cook until the edges curl and the surface are no longer wet, about 2-3 minutes per side. Repeat with the remaining batter.
5. In a separate mixing bowl, beat the chilled coconut milk, maple syrup, and vanilla extract until it thickens and resembles whipped cream.
6. Fill each crepe with a handful of mixed berries and a dollop of coconut whipped cream. Roll up and serve immediately.

Nutritional Values: Calories: 308kcal Fat: 19g Carbohydrates: 28g Fiber: 3g Protein: 5g

29. Breakfast Pita Pocket with Scrambled Eggs, Spinach, And Feta Cheese

Preparation time: 10 minutes **Cooking Time:** 10 minutes **Servings:** 2 **Difficulty:** Easy
Ingredients:
- 2 gluten-free, low FODMAP pita bread
- 4 eggs
- 1 cup baby spinach
- 1/4 cup crumbled feta cheese
- 1 tbsp. olive oil
- Salt and pepper to taste

Instructions:
1. Heat a skillet over medium heat and add the olive oil.
2. Whisk the eggs with salt and pepper in a small bowl to taste.
3. Add the whisked eggs to the skillet and scramble until fully cooked.
4. Remove the eggs from the skillet and set aside.
5. Add the baby spinach and sauté until wilted in the same skillet.
6. Warm the pita bread in the microwave for 10-15 seconds.
7. Cut the pita bread in half to create pockets.
8. Stuff each pita pocket with scrambled eggs and sautéed spinach.
9. Top with crumbled feta cheese.
10. Serve and enjoy!

Nutritional Values: Calories: 330 Fat: 18g Carbohydrates: 25g Fiber: 3g Protein: 18g Sodium: 450mg Potassium: 186mg Sugar: 1g

30. Breakfast Hash with Sweet Potato, Turkey Sausage, And Bell Peppers

Preparation time: 10 minutes **Cooking Time:** 25 minutes **Servings:** 4 **Difficulty:** Easy
Ingredients:

- 1 large, sweet potato, peeled and diced.
- 2 tbsp olive oil
- 4 turkey sausages, sliced.
- 1 red bell pepper, diced.
- 1 green bell pepper, diced.
- Salt and pepper, to taste
- 4 eggs

Instructions:

1. Preheat the oven to 400°F (200°C).
2. Toss the diced sweet potato with 1 tablespoon of olive oil and spread in a single layer on a baking sheet. Roast for 20-25 minutes or until tender and golden brown.
3. Heat the olive oil in a large skillet over medium heat. Add the sliced turkey sausage and sauté for 3-5 minutes or until browned.
4. Add the diced bell peppers to the skillet and sauté for 2-3 minutes or until tender.
5. Add the roasted sweet potato to the skillet and season with salt and pepper to taste. Stir to combine and cook for an additional 2-3 minutes.
6. Crack the eggs over the hash and cover the skillet. Cook for 5-7 minutes or until the eggs are set to your desired level of doneness.
7. Serve hot.

Nutritional Values: Calories: 347kcal Fat: 22g Carbohydrates: 19g Fiber: 3g Protein: 20g

31. Breakfast Muffin with Turkey Bacon and Cheddar Cheese

Preparation time: 15 minutes **Cooking Time:** 25 minutes **Servings:** 6 **Difficulty:** Easy
Ingredients:

- 1 cup gluten-free all-purpose flour
- 1/4 cup almond flour
- 1 tablespoon baking powder
- 1/4 teaspoon salt
- 1/4 teaspoon black pepper
- 2 large eggs
- 1/2 cup lactose-free milk
- 1/4 cup olive oil
- 4 slices turkey bacon cooked and chopped.
- 1/2 cup shredded cheddar cheese
- 2 tablespoons chopped fresh chives.

Instructions:

1. Preheat the oven to 375°F (190°C) and grease a muffin tin.
2. Combine the gluten-free all-purpose flour, almond flour, baking powder, salt, and black pepper in a mixing bowl.
3. Whisk the eggs, lactose-free milk, and olive oil until smooth in another mixing bowl.
4. Gradually add the dry ingredients to the wet ingredients, stirring until well combined.
5. Fold the chopped turkey bacon, shredded cheddar cheese, and chopped fresh chives.
6. Spoon the batter into the prepared muffin tin, filling each muffin cup about 2/3 full.
7. Bake for 25 minutes or until a toothpick inserted into the center of a muffin comes out clean.

8. Remove the muffin tin from the oven and allow it to cool in the tin for a few minutes before removing them to a wire rack to cool completely.

Nutritional Values: Calories: 250 kcal Fat: 17g Carbohydrates: 17g Fiber: 2g Protein: 7g

32. Breakfast Tart with Goat Cheese and Caramelized Onions

Cooking Time: 20 minutes **Servings:** 12 muffins **Difficulty:** Easy

Ingredients:
- 1 cup gluten-free all-purpose flour
- 1 cup almond flour
- 1 tsp baking powder
- 1/2 tsp baking soda
- 1/2 tsp salt
- 1/2 tsp black pepper
- 1/4 cup unsalted butter, melted.
- 1/2 cup lactose-free milk
- 2 large eggs
- 4 slices of turkey bacon cooked and chopped.
- 1/2 cup shredded cheddar cheese
- 2 tbsp chopped fresh chives.

Instructions:
1. Preheat the oven to 375°F and line a tin with muffin liners.
2. Mix the gluten-free all-purpose flour, almond flour, baking powder, baking soda, salt, and black pepper in a large bowl.
3. Whisk together the melted butter, lactose-free milk, and eggs in a separate bowl.
4. Add the wet and dry ingredients to mix until just combined.

5. Fold in the cooked turkey bacon, shredded cheddar cheese, and chopped fresh chives.
6. Spoon the batter evenly into the prepared muffin tin.
7. Bake for 20 minutes or until a toothpick inserted into the center of a muffin comes out clean.
8. Let the muffins cool in the tin for 5 minutes before transferring them to a wire rack to cool completely.

Nutritional Values: Calories: 150 kcal Fat: 10g Carbohydrates: 10g Fiber: 2g Protein: 6g

33. Breakfast Casserole with Spinach and Feta Cheese

Preparation time: 15 minutes **Cooking Time:** 1-hour **Servings:** 6-8 **Difficulty:** Medium

Ingredients:
- 1 gluten-free pie crust
- 1 tablespoon olive oil
- 2 large, sweet onions, thinly sliced.
- 1/4 teaspoon salt
- 1/4 teaspoon black pepper
- 4 ounces goat cheese, crumbled.
- 4 large eggs
- 1/2 cup lactose-free milk
- 1 tablespoon chopped fresh thyme leaves.

Instructions:
1. Preheat the oven to 350°F.
2. Roll out the pie crust on a lightly floured surface and place it in a 9-inch tart pan. Prick the bottom with a fork and bake for 10-12 minutes or until lightly golden. Set aside to cool.
3. Heat the olive oil over medium heat in a large skillet. Add the sliced onions, salt, and black pepper, and cook until the

onions are caramelized and golden brown, stirring occasionally, about 25-30 minutes. Set aside to cool.

4. Whisk together the eggs, lactose-free milk, and chopped thyme leaves in a medium bowl. Season with salt and black pepper.

5. Spread the caramelized onions evenly over the bottom of the baked crust. Next, sprinkle the crumbled goat cheese over the onions.

6. Pour the egg mixture over the onions and cheese.

7. Bake for 35-40 minutes until the egg mixture is set and the top is golden brown.

8. Let cool for 10-15 minutes before slicing and serving.

Nutritional Values: Calories: 263kcal Fat: 16g Saturated Fat: 7g Cholesterol: 121mg Sodium: 295mg

Potassium: 180mg Carbohydrates: 19g Fiber: 2g Sugar: 5g Protein: 9g

34. Breakfast Casserole with Spinach and Feta Cheese

Preparation time: 15 minutes **Cooking Time:** 50 minutes **Servings:** 8 **Difficulty:** Easy
Ingredients:

- 1 lb. ground turkey sausage
- 1 tbsp olive oil
- 4 cups fresh spinach, chopped.
- 8 eggs
- 1 cup lactose-free milk
- 1 tsp salt
- 1/2 tsp black pepper
- 1/2 cup crumbled feta cheese

Instructions:

1. Preheat the oven to 375°F (190°C). Grease a 9x13-inch baking dish with cooking spray.

2. In a large skillet over medium-high heat, cook the turkey sausage until browned and no longer pink. Remove from the pan and set aside.

3. Add the olive oil to the same skillet and cook the spinach until wilted about 3-4 minutes. Remove from heat and set aside.

4. In a large bowl, whisk the eggs, lactose-free milk, salt, and black pepper until well combined.

5. Stir in the cooked sausage and spinach, then pour the mixture into the prepared baking dish.

6. Sprinkle the crumbled feta cheese on top of the egg mixture.

7. Bake for 35-40 minutes until the center is set and the edges are golden brown.

8. Let the casserole cool briefly before slicing and serving.

Nutritional Values: Calories: 235kcal Fat: 15g Carbohydrates: 3g Protein: 20g Fiber: 0g

35. Blueberry Muffins with Almond Flour and Coconut Milk:

Preparation time: 15 minutes **Cooking Time:** 25 minutes **Servings:** 12 muffins **Difficulty:** Easy
Ingredients:

- 2 cups almond flour
- 1/2 cup coconut flour
- 1/2 cup maple syrup
- 1 tsp baking soda
- 1/2 tsp salt
- 3 eggs

- 1/2 cup coconut milk
- 1/4 cup melted coconut oil.
- 1 tsp vanilla extract
- 1 cup fresh blueberries

Instructions:

1. Preheat the oven to 350°F (175°C).
2. Whisk together the almond flour, coconut flour, baking soda, and salt in a large mixing bowl.
3. Whisk together the eggs, coconut milk, melted coconut oil, maple syrup, and vanilla extract in a separate mixing bowl.
4. Pour the wet ingredients into the dry ingredients and stir until well combined.
5. Fold in the blueberries.
6. Grease a muffin tin with cooking spray or line it with muffin liners.
7. Spoon the batter evenly into each muffin cup.
8. Bake for 20-25 minutes or until a toothpick comes out clean.
9. Allow the muffins to cool in the tin for 5 minutes before transferring them to a wire rack to cool completely.

Nutritional Values: Calories: 226 kcal Fat: 16.5g Carbohydrates: 16.9g Fiber: 3.8g Protein: 6.2g

Lunch

36. Turkey And Spinach Wrap with Avocado Mayo

Preparation time: 10 minutes **Servings:** 2
Difficulty: Easy
Ingredients:
- 4 gluten-free low FODMAP tortillas
- 1/2 lb. turkey breast, sliced.
- 2 cups spinach leaves
- 1 avocado
- 1 tbsp mayonnaise
- 1 tbsp lime juice
- 1/4 tsp salt
- 1/4 tsp black pepper

Instructions:
1. In a small bowl, mash the avocado with a fork.
2. Add the mayonnaise, lime juice, salt, and black pepper to the mashed avocado, and mix well to combine.
3. Spread a generous amount of avocado mayo on each tortilla.
4. Divide the sliced turkey, and spinach leaves evenly among the tortillas.
5. Roll up the tortillas tightly and cut them in half.

Nutritional Values: Calories: 342 Fat: 14g Carbohydrates: 29g Fiber: 7g Protein: 25g

37. Quinoa And Black Bean Salad with Cilantro and Lime Dressing

Preparation time: 15 minutes **Cooking Time:** 20 minutes **Servings:** 4-6 **Difficulty:** Easy
Ingredients:
- 1 cup quinoa rinsed and drained.
- 1 can black beans rinsed and drained.
- 1 red bell pepper, diced.
- 2 green onions thinly sliced.
- 1/4 cup chopped fresh cilantro.
- 2 tablespoons fresh lime juice
- 2 tablespoons olive oil
- 1 teaspoon ground cumin
- 1/2 teaspoon chili powder
- Salt and pepper to taste

Instructions:
1. Cook the quinoa according to the package instructions. Once cooked, remove from heat and fluff with a fork.
2. Combine the cooked quinoa, black beans, diced red bell pepper, sliced green onions, and chopped cilantro in a large bowl.
3. Whisk together the lime juice, olive oil, cumin, chili powder, salt, and pepper in a separate small bowl.
4. Pour the dressing over the quinoa mixture and toss to coat evenly.
5. Serve immediately or refrigerate until ready to serve.

Nutritional Values: Calories: 235 kcal Fat: 8g Carbohydrates: 34g Fiber: 8g Protein: 9g

38. Chicken And Vegetable Stir-Fry with Brown Rice

Preparation time: 10 minutes **Cooking Time:** 20 minutes **Servings:** 4 **Difficulty:** Easy
Ingredients:
- 1-pound boneless, skinless chicken breasts, sliced
- 1 tablespoon olive oil
- 1 red bell pepper, sliced.
- 1 green bell pepper, sliced.
- 1 cup sliced carrots.

- 1 cup sliced zucchini.
- 1 cup sliced green beans.
- 1/4 cup gluten-free, low FODMAP soy sauce
- 2 tablespoons rice vinegar
- 2 tablespoons brown sugar
- 1 teaspoon ground ginger
- 1 teaspoon garlic powder
- 1 tablespoon cornstarch
- 2 tablespoons water
- 4 cups cooked brown rice.

Instructions:

1. Heat the olive oil in a large skillet over medium-high heat.
2. Add the chicken and cook for 5-6 minutes until browned and cooked. Remove from the skillet and set aside.
3. Add the bell peppers, carrots, zucchini, and green beans to the skillet and sauté for 5-7 minutes until tender.
4. Whisk together the soy sauce, rice vinegar, brown sugar, ginger, and garlic powder in a small bowl.
5. In another small bowl, whisk together the cornstarch and water.
6. Add the chicken back to the skillet with the vegetables.
7. Pour the soy sauce mixture over the chicken and vegetables and stir to combine.
8. Add the cornstarch mixture to the skillet and start to thicken the sauce.
9. Serve the stir-fry over cooked brown rice.

Nutritional Values: Calories: 391 kcal Carbohydrates: 44g Protein: 31g Fat: 10g Saturated Fat: 2g Cholesterol: 73mg Sodium: 746mg Potassium: 778mg Fiber: 6g Sugar: 9g Vitamin A: 9096IU Vitamin C: 57mg Calcium: 74mg Iron: 2mg

39. Egg Salad With Lettuce and Bread

Preparation time: 10 minutes **Cooking Time:** 10 minutes (for boiling eggs) **Servings:** 2-3 **Difficulty:** Easy

Ingredients:
- 4 large eggs
- 2 tbsp lactose-free mayonnaise
- 1 tbsp Dijon mustard
- 2 tbsp chopped scallions (green parts only)
- 1 tbsp chopped fresh dill.
- 1/4 tsp salt
- 1/8 tsp black pepper
- 4-6 large lettuce leaves
- 4 slices of gluten-free bread

Instructions:

1. Fill a medium pot with water and boil over high heat. Once boiling, add the eggs and cook for 10 minutes.
2. While the eggs are cooking, prepare the other ingredients. Chop the scallions and dill and set aside.
3. Mix the mayonnaise, Dijon mustard, chopped scallions, chopped dill, salt, and pepper in a medium bowl.
4. Once the eggs are cooked, remove them from the pot and place them in a bowl of cold water to cool for a few minutes.
5. Once the eggs are cool, peel them and chop them into small pieces.
6. Add the chopped eggs to the bowl with the mayonnaise mixture and stir until well combined.
7. To assemble the sandwiches, place a lettuce leaf on each slice of gluten-free bread and spoon the egg salad on top.
8. Serve immediately.

Nutritional Values: Calories: 227 Fat: 12.5g Carbohydrates: 17g Fiber: 2g Protein: 11g Sodium: 537mg

40. Kale And Quinoa Salad with Cherry Tomatoes and Feta Cheese

Preparation time: 15 minutes **Cooking Time:** 20-25 minutes **Servings:** 4 **Difficulty:** Easy
Ingredients:
- 1 cup quinoa, rinsed.
- 2 cups water or low-FODMAP chicken broth
- 4 cups kale, chopped.
- 1-pint cherry tomatoes, halved
- 4 oz feta cheese, crumbled.
- 1/4 cup chopped walnuts.
- 2 tbsp olive oil
- 1 tbsp red wine vinegar
- Salt and pepper to taste

Instructions:
1. Cook the quinoa according to package instructions, using water or low-FODMAP chicken broth instead of regular water.
2. While the quinoa is cooking, chop the kale and place it in a large mixing bowl.
3. Add the cherry tomatoes, crumbled feta cheese, and chopped walnuts to the mixing bowl.
4. Whisk together the olive oil and red wine vinegar in a separate small bowl to make the dressing.
5. Once the quinoa is finished cooking, let it cool for a few minutes before adding it to the mixing bowl with the other ingredients.
6. Pour the dressing over the salad and toss everything together until the kale and quinoa are well-coated.
7. Season with salt and pepper to taste and serve immediately.

Nutritional Values: Calories: 350 Fat: 18g Carbohydrates: 36g Fiber: 6g Protein: 12g

41. Veggie Burger with Sweet Potato Fries

Preparation time: 20 minutes **Cooking Time:** 30 minutes **Servings:** 4 **Difficulty:** Easy
Ingredients:
For the veggie burger:
- 1 cup cooked quinoa
- 1 can (15 oz) black beans, drained and rinsed.
- 1/2 cup gluten-free breadcrumbs
- 1/4 cup finely chopped red onion.
- 1/4 cup finely chopped bell pepper.
- 1 egg
- 1 tsp ground cumin
- 1/2 tsp smoked paprika.
- 1/4 tsp garlic powder
- Salt and pepper, to taste
- 4 gluten-free hamburger buns

For the sweet potato fries:
- 2 medium sweet potatoes, peeled and cut into thin fries.
- 2 tbsp olive oil
- 1/2 tsp paprika
- Salt and pepper, to taste

Instructions:
1. Preheat the oven to 400°F.
2. In a large bowl, mash the black beans with a fork or potato masher.
3. Add the cooked quinoa, gluten-free breadcrumbs, red onion, bell pepper, egg, cumin, smoked paprika, garlic

powder, salt, and pepper to the bowl. Mix until well combined.

4. Form the mixture into four patties.
5. Heat a large skillet over medium heat. Add a little oil to the pan and cook the patties for 4-5 minutes on each side or until golden brown.
6. While the patties are cooking, prepare the sweet potato fries. Toss the sweet potato fries with olive oil, paprika, salt, and pepper in a large bowl.
7. Spread the sweet potato fries in a single layer on a baking sheet. Bake in the oven for 20-25 minutes or until crispy and golden brown.
8. Toast the gluten-free hamburger buns.
9. Serve the veggie burger patties on the toasted buns with lettuce, tomato, and any other toppings you like. Serve with the sweet potato fries on the side.

Nutritional Values: Calories: 493 Fat: 18g Carbohydrates: 70g Fiber: 14g Protein: 16g

42. Chicken Caesar Salad with Gluten-Free Croutons

Preparation time: 15 minutes **Cooking Time:** 20 minutes **Servings:** 4 **Difficulty:** Easy
Ingredients:
For the croutons:
- 4 slices of gluten-free bread, cut into cubes.
- 2 tablespoons of olive oil
- 1/2 teaspoon of garlic powder
- Salt and pepper to taste
For the salad:
- 2 heads of romaine lettuce washed and chopped.
- 1 pound of boneless, skinless chicken breasts cooked and chopped.
- 1/4 cup of grated Parmesan cheese

- 1/4 cup of gluten-free Caesar dressing
- Salt and pepper to taste

Instructions:
1. Preheat your oven to 375°F (190°C).
2. Toss the bread cubes with olive oil, garlic powder, salt, and pepper in a bowl.
3. Spread the bread cubes on a baking sheet and bake for 15-20 minutes or until crispy.
4. Combine the romaine lettuce, chopped chicken, and Parmesan cheese in a large bowl.
5. Drizzle Caesar dressing over the salad and toss to coat.
6. Divide the salad evenly among 4 plates and top each with the gluten-free croutons.

Nutritional Values: Calories: 350 kcal Fat: 19 g Carbohydrates: 16 g Fiber: 4 g Protein: 30 g

43. Roasted Vegetable and Goat Cheese Quiche

Preparation time: 30 minutes **Cooking Time:** 45-50 minutes **Servings:** 6-8 **Difficulty:** Medium
Ingredients:
For the crust:
- 1 cup gluten-free all-purpose flour
- 1/4 teaspoon salt
- 1/4 cup unsalted butter, chilled and diced.
- 2-3 tablespoons ice water
For the filling:
- 1 medium zucchini, sliced.
- 1 red bell pepper, sliced.
- 1 yellow onion, sliced.
- 2 tablespoons olive oil
- Salt and pepper, to taste
- 4 large eggs

- 1/2 cup lactose-free milk
- 1/2 cup crumbled goat cheese
- 1 tablespoon chopped fresh parsley.
- 1 tablespoon chopped fresh chives.

Instructions:

1. Preheat the oven to 375°F (190°C).
2. Whisk together the gluten-free flour and salt in a mixing bowl to make the crust. Cut in the diced butter using a pastry blender or your fingertips until the mixture resembles coarse sand.
3. Add ice water, 1 tablespoon, and mix until the dough comes together in a ball.
4. Flatten the dough into a disc and wrap it in plastic wrap. Refrigerate for at least 30 minutes.
5. Roll the dough on a lightly floured surface to fit a 9-inch pie dish. Place the dough in the container and trim the edges. Prick the bottom of the crust with a fork and bake for 10-12 minutes, until slightly golden. Remove from the oven and set aside.
6. Increase the oven temperature to 400°F (200°C).
7. Toss the zucchini, red bell pepper, and onion in olive oil and season with salt and pepper. Spread the vegetables on a baking sheet and roast for 15-20 minutes until tender and slightly charred. Remove from the oven and set aside.
8. Whisk together the eggs, lactose-free milk, goat cheese, parsley, and chives in a mixing bowl.
9. Pour the egg mixture into the pre-baked crust. Arrange the roasted vegetables on top of the egg mixture.
10. Bake the quiche for 25-30 minutes until the filling is set and slightly golden.

Remove from the oven and let it cool for 5-10 minutes before serving.

Nutritional Values: Calories: 243kcal Fat: 16g Carbohydrates: 17g Fiber: 2g Sugar: 2g Protein: 8g

44. Zucchini Noodles with Turkey Meatballs and Tomato Sauce

Preparation time: 15 minutes **Cooking Time:** 25 minutes **Servings:** 4 **Difficulty:** Easy

Ingredients:

For the turkey meatballs:

- 1 lb. ground turkey
- 1/4 cup gluten-free breadcrumbs
- 1/4 cup chopped fresh parsley.
- 1 egg
- 1/2 tsp salt
- 1/4 tsp black pepper
- 1 tbsp olive oil

For the tomato sauce:

- 1 can (28 oz) crushed tomatoes
- 1/4 cup chopped fresh basil.
- 1 tsp dried oregano
- 1/4 tsp salt
- 1/4 tsp black pepper

For the zucchini noodles:

- 4 medium zucchinis
- 2 tbsp olive oil
- 2 cloves garlic, minced.
- 1/4 tsp salt
- 1/4 tsp black pepper

Instructions:

1. Preheat the oven to 375°F (190°C). Line a baking sheet with parchment paper.
2. Mix the ground turkey, breadcrumbs, parsley, egg, salt, and pepper in a large bowl until well combined.
3. Form the mixture into 16 meatballs.

4. Heat the olive oil in a large skillet over medium heat. Add the meatballs and cook, turning occasionally, until browned on all sides, about 8 minutes. Transfer the meatballs to the prepared baking sheet and bake for 10-12 minutes or until cooked.

5. While the meatballs are baking, make the tomato sauce. Combine the crushed tomatoes, basil, oregano, salt, and pepper in a medium saucepan. Bring to a simmer over medium heat and let cook for 10 minutes.

6. Use a spiralizer or vegetable peeler to make zucchini noodles.

7. In a large skillet, heat the olive oil over medium heat. Add the garlic and cook for 1 minute or until fragrant. Add the zucchini noodles, salt, and pepper and cook, stirring occasionally, for 2-3 minutes or until tender.

8. Serve the zucchini noodles with the turkey meatballs and tomato sauce.

Nutritional Values: Calories: 314 Fat: 16g Carbohydrates: 18g Fiber: 5g Protein: 25g Sodium: 783mg

45. Tomato And Mozzarella Salad with Basil and Balsamic Vinaigrette

Preparation time: 10 minutes **Cooking Time:** N/A **Servings:** 4 **Difficulty:** Easy
Ingredients:
- 2 medium-sized tomatoes, sliced.
- 8 oz fresh mozzarella cheese, sliced.
- 1/4 cup fresh basil leaves, torn.
- 2 tbsp balsamic vinegar
- 1 tbsp olive oil
- 1 tsp Dijon mustard

- Salt and pepper to taste

Instructions:
1. Arrange the sliced tomatoes and mozzarella cheese on a serving platter.
2. Sprinkle torn basil leaves over the tomatoes and cheese.
3. Whisk together balsamic vinegar, olive oil, Dijon mustard, salt, and pepper in a small bowl to make the vinaigrette.
4. Drizzle the vinaigrette over the salad and serve.

Nutritional Values: Calories: 190 kcal Carbohydrates: 4 g Protein: 12 g Fat: 14 g Fiber: 1 g Sodium: 330 mg

46. Sushi Roll with Tuna, Avocado, And Soy Sauce

Preparation time: 30 minutes **Cooking Time:** 15 minutes **Servings:** 4 **Difficulty:** Medium
Ingredients:
- 4 sheets of nori seaweed
- 2 cups of cooked sushi rice
- 8 oz of sushi-grade tuna, sliced into thin strips.
- 1 avocado, sliced.
- 1 cucumber, seeded and cut into thin strips.
- 2 tablespoons of pickled ginger
- 2 tablespoons of gluten-free soy sauce
- Wasabi paste (optional)
- Bamboo sushi rolling mat.

Instructions:
1. Rinse the sushi rice several times with cold water until the water runs clear. Cook according to package instructions and let it cool.
2. Lay a nori sheet on the sushi rolling mat with the shiny side facing down.
3. Spread a thin layer of rice over the nori,

leaving about 1 inch at the top edge uncovered.

4. Arrange the sliced tuna, avocado, and cucumber on top of the rice horizontally, about 1 inch from the bottom edge of the nori.

5. Add a small amount of pickled ginger on top of the filling.

6. Wet the uncovered edge of the nori with water using your fingertips or a brush.

7. Hold the ingredients in place with your fingers and use the mat to roll the sushi tightly from the bottom to the top edge, pressing down firmly to seal the roll.

8. Repeat the process with the remaining nori sheets and ingredients.

9. Use a sharp knife to slice each roll into 6-8 pieces.

10. Serve with gluten-free soy sauce and wasabi paste on the side.

Nutritional Values: Calories: 320 kcal Protein: 22 g Fat: 12 g Carbohydrates: 28 g Fiber: 4 g Sugar: 1 g Sodium: 390 mg

47. Chicken And Vegetable Soup with Gluten-Free Noodles

Preparation time: 15 minutes **Cooking Time:** 30 minutes **Servings:** 4-6 **Difficulty:** Easy
Ingredients:
- 1 tablespoon garlic-infused oil
- 1-pound boneless, skinless chicken breasts cut into small pieces
- 2 medium carrots peeled and diced.
- 2 stalks of celery, diced.
- 1 zucchini, diced.
- 1 teaspoon dried thyme
- 4 cups low FODMAP chicken broth
- 1 cup gluten-free noodles
- Salt and pepper to taste
- Chopped fresh parsley for garnish.

Instructions:
1. Heat the garlic-infused oil in a large pot over medium-high heat.

2. Add the chicken and cook until browned on all sides, about 5-7 minutes.

3. Add the carrots, celery, zucchini, and thyme, and cook until the vegetables are slightly softened about 5-7 minutes.

4. Add the chicken broth and bring to a simmer. Simmer for 15-20 minutes or until the vegetables are tender.

5. Add the gluten-free noodles and cook until al dente, according to package instructions.

6. Season with salt and pepper to taste.

7. Serve hot, garnished with chopped fresh parsley.

Nutritional Values: Calories: 193kcal Fat: 4g Carbohydrates: 12g Fiber: 1g Protein: 27g

48. Vegetable And Tofu Stir-Fry with Brown Rice

Preparation time: 10 minutes **Cooking Time:** 20 minutes **Servings:** 4 **Difficulty:** Easy
Ingredients:
- 2 cups of cooked brown rice
- 2 tablespoons of olive oil
- 1 block of firm tofu, cubed.
- 1 red bell pepper, sliced.
- 1 yellow bell pepper, sliced.
- 1 zucchini, sliced.
- 1 cup of broccoli florets
- 1 cup of sliced carrots
- 1/2 cup of low FODMAP stir-fry sauce
- 2 tablespoons of sesame seeds (optional)

For the stir-fry sauce:
- 1/2 cup of low-sodium soy sauce
- 1/4 cup of maple syrup
- 1/4 cup of rice vinegar

- 1 teaspoon of grated ginger
- 1 teaspoon of garlic-infused oil

Instructions:

1. Mix all the ingredients for the stir-fry sauce in a small bowl.
2. Heat the olive oil in a large skillet or wok over medium-high heat.
3. Add the cubed tofu and stir-fry for 3-4 minutes or until lightly browned.
4. Add the sliced bell peppers, zucchini, broccoli florets, and sliced carrots to the skillet. Stir-fry for 5-7 minutes or until the vegetables are tender-crisp.
5. Pour the stir-fry sauce over the vegetables and tofu, stirring to coat evenly.
6. Cook for another 2-3 minutes or until the sauce has thickened.
7. Serve the vegetable and tofu stir-fry over cooked brown rice, and sprinkle with sesame seeds if desired.

Nutritional Values: Calories: 324 kcal Fat: 11 g Carbohydrates: 43 g Fiber: 5 g Protein: 14 g

49. Chicken And Pesto Salad with Mixed Greens and Gluten-Free Croutons

Preparation time: 20 minutes **Cooking Time:** None **Servings:** 2-3 **Difficulty:** Easy

Ingredients:

- 2 chicken breasts cooked and sliced.
- 4 cups mixed greens
- 1/4 cup chopped walnuts.
- 1/4 cup crumbled feta cheese
- 1/4 cup gluten-free croutons
- 1/4 cup Low FODMAP pesto (store-bought or homemade)
- 2 tablespoons olive oil
- 1 tablespoon balsamic vinegar

- Salt and pepper to taste

Instructions:

1. Combine the mixed greens, chopped walnuts, crumbled feta cheese, and gluten-free croutons in a large bowl.
2. Whisk together the Low FODMAP pesto, olive oil, balsamic vinegar, salt, and pepper in a small bowl.
3. Add the sliced chicken to the large bowl with the mixed greens and pour the pesto dressing over the top.
4. Toss everything together until well coated.
5. Serve immediately.

Nutritional Values: Calories: 389 Fat: 25g Carbohydrates: 10g Fiber: 4g Protein: 32g

50. Greek Salad with Feta Cheese, Olives, And Gluten-Free Pita Bread

Preparation time: 10 minutes **Cooking Time:** None **Servings:** 2 **Difficulty:** Easy

Ingredients:

- 2 cups mixed salad greens
- 1/2 cup cherry tomatoes, halved.
- 1/4 cup sliced cucumber.
- 1/4 cup crumbled feta cheese
- 1/4 cup kalamata olives
- 2 gluten-free pita bread
- 2 tbsp olive oil
- 1 tbsp lemon juice
- 1/2 tsp dried oregano
- Salt and pepper to taste

Instructions:

1. Preheat oven to 375°F. Cut the gluten-free pita bread into small pieces, toss with 1 tbsp olive oil, and spread out on a baking sheet. Bake for 10-12 minutes or until crispy.

2. Combine the mixed salad greens, cherry tomatoes, sliced cucumber, crumbled feta cheese, and kalamata olives in a large bowl.
3. Whisk together 1 tbsp olive oil, lemon juice, dried oregano, salt, and pepper in a small bowl to make the dressing.
4. Drizzle the dressing over the salad and toss to combine.
5. Serve the salad with the crispy gluten-free pita bread on the side.

Nutritional Values: Calories: 290 kcal Fat: 22g Carbohydrates: 18g Fiber: 3g Protein: 6g

51. Beef And Broccoli Stir-Fry with Gluten-Free Soy Sauce

Preparation time: 15 minutes **Cooking Time:** 20 minutes **Servings:** 4 **Difficulty:** Easy
Ingredients:

- 1 lb. beef sirloin sliced thinly.
- 1 lb. broccoli florets
- 2 tbsp garlic-infused oil
- 1 tbsp grated fresh ginger.
- 2 tbsp gluten-free soy sauce
- 1 tbsp rice vinegar
- 1 tsp honey
- 1 tbsp cornstarch
- Salt and pepper, to taste
- Green onions, sliced (optional)

Instructions:

1. Mix the gluten-free soy sauce, rice vinegar, honey, and cornstarch in a small bowl. Set aside.
2. Heat the garlic-infused oil in a large skillet or wok over high heat.
3. Add the beef to the skillet and stir-fry for 2-3 minutes, until browned.
4. Add the broccoli and grated ginger to the skillet and stir-fry for 5-6 minutes until the broccoli is tender but still crisp.

5. Pour the soy sauce mixture over the beef and broccoli and stir to combine.
6. Cook for 2-3 minutes, until the sauce thickens, and the beef is cooked through.
7. Season with salt and pepper to taste and top with sliced green onions, if desired.
8. Serve hot with gluten-free rice or noodles.

Nutritional Values: Calories: 259 kcal Protein: 28 g Fat: 12 g Carbohydrates: 10 g Fiber: 3 g Sugar: 4 g Sodium: 570 mg

52. Baked Sweet Potato with Turkey Chili and Avocado

Preparation time: 15 minutes **Cooking Time:** 1-hour **Servings:** 4 **Difficulty:** Easy
Ingredients:

- 4 medium sweet potatoes
- 1 tablespoon olive oil
- 1 small onion, chopped.
- 1 red bell pepper, chopped.
- 1 lb. ground turkey
- 1 can (14 oz) diced tomatoes.
- 1 can (14 oz) kidney beans, drained and rinsed.
- 1 tablespoon chili powder
- 1 teaspoon cumin
- 1/2 teaspoon smoked paprika.
- Salt and pepper, to taste
- 1 avocado, diced.
- 1/4 cup chopped fresh cilantro.

Instructions:

1. Preheat the oven to 400°F (200°C).
2. Scrub the sweet potatoes and pierce them a few times with a fork. Place them on a baking sheet and bake for 45-50 minutes or until tender.
3. While the sweet potatoes are baking, heat the olive oil in a large skillet over

medium-high heat. Add the onion, red bell pepper, and sauté for 2-3 minutes, or until the onion is translucent.

4. Add the ground turkey to the skillet and cook, breaking it up with a wooden spoon, until it is browned and cooked through about 5-7 minutes.

5. Add the diced tomatoes, kidney beans, chili powder, cumin, smoked paprika, salt, and pepper to the skillet. Stir to combine and bring to a simmer. Cook for 10-15 minutes or until the flavors have melded together and the chili has thickened.

6. Once the sweet potatoes are done baking, remove them from the oven and let them cool for a few minutes.

7. Cut a slit down the middle of each sweet potato and gently press the ends together to open a pocket.

8. Spoon the turkey chili into the sweet potato pockets, then top with diced avocado and chopped cilantro.

Nutritional Values: Calories: 452 kcal Fat: 21 g Carbohydrates: 38 g Fiber: 12 g Protein: 31 g Sodium: 605 mg

53.Chicken And Vegetable Kebabs with Gluten-Free Tzatziki Sauce

Preparation time: 20 minutes **Cooking Time:** 20 minutes **Servings:** 4 **Difficulty:** Easy
Ingredients:
For the kebabs:
- 1 lb. boneless, skinless chicken breasts cut into bite-sized pieces.
- 1 zucchini, sliced into rounds.
- 1 red bell pepper, seeded and cut into bite-sized pieces.
- 1 yellow onion, cut into bite-sized pieces.
- 8 wooden skewers, soaked in water for 30 minutes.

For the marinade:
- 1/4 cup olive oil
- 2 tablespoons lemon juice
- 2 tablespoons chopped fresh oregano.
- 1 tablespoon Dijon mustard
- 1 teaspoon salt
- 1/2 teaspoon black pepper

For the tzatziki sauce:
- 1 cup plain lactose-free yogurt
- 1/2 cup peeled and grated cucumber.
- 1 tablespoon chopped fresh dill.
- 1 tablespoon lemon juice
- Salt and pepper to taste

Instructions:
1. Whisk together the olive oil, lemon juice, oregano, mustard, salt, and black pepper in a large bowl. Add the chicken, zucchini, bell pepper, and onion, and toss to coat in the marinade. Cover and refrigerate for at least 30 minutes or up to 2 hours.

2. Preheat the grill to medium-high heat.

3. Thread the chicken and vegetables onto the skewers, alternating between each ingredient.

4. Grill the kebabs for 10-12 minutes, turning occasionally, until the chicken is cooked, and the vegetables are tender.

5. Meanwhile, in a small bowl, prepare the tzatziki sauce by combining the yogurt, grated cucumber, dill, lemon juice, salt, and pepper. Stir to combine.

6. Serve the kebabs hot, with the tzatziki sauce on the side for dipping.

Nutritional Values: Calories: 321kcal Fat: 17g Carbohydrates: 9g Fiber: 2g Protein: 32g

54. Roasted Beet and Goat Cheese Salad with Mixed Greens And Walnuts

Preparation time: 20 minutes **Cooking Time:** 45 minutes **Servings:** 4 **Difficulty:** Easy
Ingredients:

- 4 medium beets, peeled and chopped into 1-inch cubes.
- 2 tablespoons olive oil
- Salt and pepper to taste
- 4 cups mixed greens
- 4 ounces goat cheese, crumbled.
- 1/2 cup walnuts, chopped.

For the dressing:

- 2 tablespoons olive oil
- 1 tablespoon balsamic vinegar
- 1 teaspoon Dijon mustard
- Salt and pepper to taste

Instructions:

1. Preheat the oven to 400°F.
2. Toss the chopped beets with olive oil, salt, and pepper in a large bowl.
3. Spread the beets out in a single layer on a baking sheet and roast for 40-45 minutes or until tender.
4. While the beets are roasting, make the dressing. Whisk together the olive oil, balsamic vinegar, Dijon mustard, salt, and pepper in a small bowl until well combined.
5. Combine the mixed greens, roasted beets, crumbled goat cheese, and chopped walnuts in a large bowl.
6. Drizzle the dressing over the salad and toss to combine.
7. Serve immediately.

Nutritional Values: Calories: 330 kcal Fat: 29g Carbohydrates: 12g Fiber: 3g Protein: 8g

55. Eggplant Roll-Ups with Ricotta Cheese and Tomato Sauce

Preparation time: 20 minutes **Cooking Time:** 30 minutes **Servings:** 4 **Difficulty:** Easy
Ingredients:

- 1 medium-sized eggplant
- 1 cup lactose-free ricotta cheese
- 1/4 cup chopped fresh parsley.
- 1/4 cup grated parmesan cheese.
- 1/4 tsp dried oregano
- 1/4 tsp salt
- 1/4 tsp black pepper
- 1 cup low FODMAP tomato sauce
- 1 tbsp olive oil

Instructions:

1. Preheat the oven to 375°F.
2. Slice the eggplant lengthwise into thin slices, about 1/4 inch thick.
3. Mix the ricotta cheese, parsley, parmesan cheese, oregano, salt, and black pepper in a medium-sized bowl.
4. Spread 1-2 tablespoons of the ricotta mixture onto each eggplant slice.
5. Carefully roll the eggplant slices and place them seam-side down in a baking dish.
6. Drizzle the olive oil over the eggplant roll-ups and spoon the tomato sauce.
7. Bake for 25-30 minutes until the eggplant is tender and the cheese is melted and lightly browned.
8. Serve hot and enjoy!

Nutritional Values: Calories: 210 kcal Fat: 14 g Carbohydrates: 14 g Fiber: 5 g Protein: 9 g Sodium: 410 mg

Quinoa and vegetable stir-fry with sesame sauce

Preparation time: 15 minutes **Cooking Time:** 20 minutes **Servings:** 4 **Difficulty:** Easy

Ingredients:

- 1 cup quinoa
- 2 cups water
- 2 tablespoons low FODMAP vegetable oil
- 1 red bell pepper, sliced.
- 1 yellow bell pepper, sliced.
- 1 small zucchini, sliced.
- 1 small yellow squash, sliced.
- 2 green onions, sliced (green parts only)
- 1/4 cup chopped fresh cilantro.
- 1/4 cup gluten-free soy sauce
- 1 tablespoon sesame oil
- 2 teaspoons honey
- 2 teaspoons grated fresh ginger.
- 2 cloves garlic, minced.
- 1 tablespoon cornstarch
- 1 tablespoon water

Instructions:

1. Rinse the quinoa and add it to a pot with 2 cups of water. Bring to a boil, then reduce the heat and let it simmer for 15-20 minutes, or until the quinoa is tender and the water has been absorbed.
2. While the quinoa is cooking, heat the vegetable oil in a large skillet over medium-high heat. Add the bell peppers, zucchini, and yellow squash, and cook for 5-7 minutes or until the vegetables are tender-crisp.
3. Whisk together the gluten-free soy sauce, sesame oil, honey, ginger, and garlic in a small bowl.
4. Whisk together the cornstarch and water in another small bowl to make a slurry.
5. Add the green onions and cilantro to the skillet with the vegetables. Pour the soy sauce mixture over the vegetables and stir to combine. Add the cornstarch slurry and stir until the sauce has thickened.
6. Serve the stir-fry over the cooked quinoa.

Nutritional Values: Calories: 310kcal Carbohydrates: 44g Protein: 8g Fat: 12g Saturated Fat: 1g Sodium: 947mg Potassium: 537mg Fiber: 6g Sugar: 8g Vitamin A: 2274IU Vitamin C: 90mg Calcium: 66mg Iron: 3mg

Turkey and spinach salad with cranberries and gluten-free croutons

Preparation time: 10 minutes **Cooking Time:** 5-7 minutes **Servings:** 4 **Difficulty:** Easy

Ingredients:

- 8 cups of fresh spinach
- 1 pound of sliced turkey breast
- 1/2 cup of dried cranberries
- 1/2 cup of gluten-free croutons
- 1/4 cup of chopped walnuts
- 1/4 cup of crumbled feta cheese
- 2 tablespoons of olive oil
- 2 tablespoons of balsamic vinegar
- 1 tablespoon of Dijon mustard
- Salt and pepper to taste

Instructions:

1. Preheat the oven to 350°F.
2. Place the gluten-free croutons on a baking sheet and bake for 5-7 minutes until crisp.
3. Add the spinach, sliced turkey breast, dried cranberries, chopped walnuts, and crumbled feta cheese in a large mixing bowl. Mix well.
4. Whisk together the olive oil, balsamic vinegar, Dijon mustard, salt, and pepper in a small mixing bowl to make the dressing.
5. Drizzle the dressing over the salad and toss until evenly coated.

6. Divide the salad into four bowls and top each with gluten-free croutons.

Nutritional Values: Calories: 330 Fat: 16g Carbohydrates: 16g Fiber: 3g Protein: 31g Sodium: 360mg

Turkey and Swiss cheese sandwich with lettuce and gluten-free bread

Preparation time: 10 minutes **Servings:** 1 **Difficulty:** Easy

Ingredients:
- 2 slices gluten-free bread
- 3-4 slices of low FODMAP turkey deli meat
- 1 slice Swiss cheese
- A handful of lettuce
- 1 tablespoon of mayonnaise
- 1 teaspoon of Dijon mustard

Instructions:
1. Toast the slices of gluten-free bread to your liking.
2. Spread mayonnaise and Dijon mustard on one side of each piece of bread.
3. Layer the turkey, Swiss cheese, and lettuce on one piece of bread.
4. Top with the other part of the bread and press gently.
5. Cut the sandwich in half and serve.

Nutritional Values: Calories: 365 kcal Fat: 17 g Carbohydrates: 25 g Protein: 24 g Fiber: 5 g

56. Vegetable And Rice Noodles Stir-Fried with Tamari Sauce

Preparation time: 20 minutes **Cooking Time:** 15 minutes **Servings:** 4 **Difficulty:** Easy

Ingredients:
- 8 oz gluten-free rice noodles
- 2 tbsp olive oil
- 2 garlic cloves, minced.
- 1-inch ginger, minced
- 2 cups mixed vegetables (carrots, bell peppers, zucchini, broccoli, etc.)
- 1 tbsp tamari sauce
- 1 tbsp maple syrup
- 1 tbsp rice vinegar
- 1 tsp sesame oil
- Salt and pepper, to taste
- Sesame seeds and green onions for garnish

Instructions:
1. Cook the rice noodles according to the package directions. Drain and set aside.
2. Heat the olive oil over medium-high heat in a large skillet or wok. Add the minced garlic and ginger and cook for 1-2 minutes, until fragrant.
3. Add the mixed vegetables to the skillet and stir-fry for 3-4 minutes until they soften.
4. Whisk together the tamari sauce, maple syrup, rice vinegar, and sesame oil in a small bowl.
5. Pour the sauce over the vegetables and stir to coat. Cook for another 1-2 minutes, until the vegetables are tender-crisp, and the sauce has thickened slightly.
6. Add the cooked rice noodles to the skillet and toss everything together to combine.
7. Season with salt and pepper to taste.
8. Serve hot, garnished with sesame seeds and green onions.

Nutritional Values: Calories: 258kcal Fat: 7g Carbohydrates: 44g Fiber: 4g Protein: 4g Sodium: 272mg

57. Shrimp And Vegetable Skewers with Gluten-Free Cocktail Sauce

Preparation time: 20 minutes **Cooking Time:** 8-10 minutes **Servings:** 4 **Difficulty:** Easy
Ingredients:

- 1-pound large shrimp, peeled and deveined
- 2 bell peppers, seeded and cut into 1-inch pieces.
- 1 zucchini, sliced into 1/4-inch rounds.
- 1/2 red onion, cut into 1-inch pieces.
- 2 tablespoons olive oil
- Salt and pepper, to taste
- 1/2 cup gluten-free cocktail sauce

Instructions:

1. Preheat the grill to medium-high heat.
2. Thread the shrimp, bell peppers, zucchini, and red onion onto skewers.
3. Brush the skewers with olive oil and season with salt and pepper.
4. Grill the skewers for 4-5 minutes per side or until the shrimp are cooked through, and the vegetables are tender.
5. Serve the skewers with gluten-free cocktail sauce for dipping.

Nutritional Values: Calories: 200kcal Fat: 8g Carbohydrates: 16g Fiber: 3g Protein: 18g

58. Spinach And Feta Stuffed Chicken Breasts with Roasted Vegetables

Preparation time: 20 minutes **Cooking Time:** 35 minutes **Servings:** 4 **Difficulty:** Intermediate
Ingredients:

- 4 boneless, skinless chicken breasts
- 1 cup of fresh spinach, chopped.
- 1/2 cup of crumbled feta cheese
- 1/4 cup of chopped green onions (green parts only)
- 1 tablespoon of garlic-infused olive oil
- Salt and pepper, to taste
- 4 cups of mixed vegetables (such as zucchini, bell peppers, and cherry tomatoes)
- 1 tablespoon of olive oil
- 1 teaspoon of dried oregano
- 1/2 teaspoon of garlic powder

Instructions:

1. Preheat the oven to 375°F (190°C).
2. Mix the spinach, feta cheese, and green onions in a small bowl.
3. Use a sharp knife to carefully cut a pocket in the thickest part of each chicken breast. Stuff each chicken breast with the spinach and feta mixture, using toothpicks to secure the openings.
4. Heat the garlic-infused olive oil in a large skillet over medium-high heat. Add the stuffed chicken breasts and cook for 3-4 minutes on each side or until browned.
5. Transfer the chicken breasts to a baking dish and season with salt and pepper.
6. Toss the mixed vegetables with olive oil, oregano, and garlic powder in a separate bowl. Arrange the vegetables around the chicken in the baking dish.
7. Bake for 25-30 minutes or until the chicken is cooked through and the vegetables are tender.
8. Let the chicken rest for 5 minutes before removing the toothpicks and serving.

Nutritional Values: Calories: 316kcal Fat: 14g Carbohydrates: 9g Fiber: 3g Protein: 38g Sodium: 328mg

59. Turkey And Kale Soup with Gluten-Free Noodles

Preparation time: 15 minutes **Cooking Time:** 45 minutes **Servings:** 4 **Difficulty:** Easy
Ingredients:

- 1 lb. ground turkey
- 1 tbsp olive oil
- 2 cups chopped kale.
- 2 carrots peeled and diced.
- 2 stalks of celery, diced.
- 1 small zucchini, diced.
- 6 cups low FODMAP chicken broth
- 1 cup gluten-free noodles
- 1 tsp dried thyme
- 1 tsp dried oregano
- Salt and pepper to taste

Instructions:

1. Heat the olive oil over medium-high heat in a large pot or Dutch oven. Add the ground turkey and cook until browned about 5 minutes.
2. Add the chopped kale, carrots, celery, and zucchini to the pot. Stir to combine and cook for another 5 minutes.
3. Pour the chicken broth and add the dried thyme, oregano, salt, and pepper. Stir to combine and bring the soup to a boil.
4. Reduce the heat to low and simmer the soup for 30 minutes.
5. In the meantime, cook the gluten-free noodles according to the package instructions.
6. Once the soup is done simmering, add the cooked noodles and stir to combine.
7. Serve hot and enjoy!

Nutritional Values: Calories: 320 Fat: 14g Carbohydrates: 17g Protein: 29g Fiber: 2g Sugar: 2g Sodium: 800mg

60. Chicken And Vegetable Curry with Brown Rice

Preparation time: 15 minutes **Cooking Time:** 40 minutes **Servings:** 4 **Difficulty:** Easy
Ingredients:

- 1 lb. boneless, skinless chicken breasts, cubed.
- 1 tablespoon coconut oil
- 1 teaspoon ground turmeric
- 1 teaspoon ground cumin
- 1 teaspoon ground coriander
- 1/2 teaspoon ground cinnamon
- 1/2 teaspoon ground ginger
- 1/4 teaspoon ground cardamom
- 1/4 teaspoon cayenne pepper
- 1/2 teaspoon salt
- 1 can (14 oz) diced tomatoes.
- 1 cup low FODMAP chicken broth
- 1 cup chopped carrots.
- 1 cup chopped zucchini.
- 1 cup chopped bell peppers.
- 1/2 cup chopped green onions (green parts only)
- 1/4 cup chopped fresh cilantro.
- 1 tablespoon lemon juice
- 4 cups cooked brown rice.

Instructions:

1. In a large saucepan, heat the coconut oil over medium-high heat.
2. Add the cubed chicken and cook until browned on all sides, about 5 minutes.
3. Add the turmeric, cumin, coriander, cinnamon, ginger, cardamom, cayenne pepper, and salt to the chicken and stir to coat evenly.
4. Add the diced tomatoes and chicken broth to the pan and combine.
5. Add the chopped carrots, zucchini, and

bell peppers to the pan and stir to combine.

6. Bring the mixture to a boil, then reduce the heat to low and simmer for 20-25 minutes or until the vegetables are tender and the chicken is cooked.

7. Stir in the chopped green onions, cilantro, and lemon juice.

8. Serve the chicken and vegetable curry over cooked brown rice.

Nutritional Values: Calories: 415 kcal Fat: 8.2 g Carbohydrates: 51.5 g Fiber: 8.3 g Protein: 34.5 g

61.Greek Yogurt Chicken Salad with Gluten-Free Crackers

Preparation time: 10 minutes **Cooking Time:** None **Servings:** 4 **Difficulty:** Easy
Ingredients:

- 2 cups cooked chicken breast, shredded.
- 1/2 cup Greek yogurt
- 1/4 cup finely chopped red bell pepper.
- 1/4 cup finely chopped cucumber.
- 2 tablespoons finely chopped red onion.
- 1 tablespoon lemon juice
- 1/4 teaspoon garlic powder
- Salt and pepper to taste
- Gluten-free crackers for serving.

Instructions:

1. Combine the shredded chicken, Greek yogurt, red bell pepper, cucumber, and red onion in a large mixing bowl.

2. Add in the lemon juice, garlic powder, salt, and pepper, and stir everything together until well combined.

3. Serve the chicken salad chilled with gluten-free crackers on the side.

Nutritional Values: Calories: 145 kcal Fat: 3.5 g Carbohydrates: 2.5 g Fiber: 0.5 g Protein: 26 g

62.Beef And Vegetable Stir-Fry with Gluten-Free Soy Sauce

Preparation time: 15 minutes **Cooking Time:** 20 minutes **Servings:** 4 **Difficulty:** Easy
Ingredients:

- 1 pound beef sirloin sliced thinly.
- 1 red bell pepper, sliced.
- 1 green bell pepper, sliced.
- 1 cup sliced carrots.
- 1 cup sliced zucchini.
- 1 tablespoon garlic-infused oil
- 1 tablespoon grated ginger
- 1/4 cup low FODMAP gluten-free soy sauce
- 1 tablespoon cornstarch
- 1/4 cup green onions, chopped.
- 2 tablespoons sesame seeds
- Salt and pepper, to taste

Instructions:

1. Mix the gluten-free soy sauce, cornstarch, and ginger in a small bowl until well combined. Set aside.

2. Heat the garlic-infused oil in a large skillet or wok over medium-high heat.

3. Add the beef and cook until browned on all sides, about 5-7 minutes.

4. Add the sliced bell peppers, carrots, and zucchini to the skillet and stir-fry for another 5-7 minutes until the vegetables are slightly tender.

5. Pour the soy sauce mixture over the beef and vegetables and stir well to coat.

6. Cook for an additional 2-3 minutes until the sauce has thickened.

7. Add salt and pepper to taste.

8. Garnish with chopped green onions and sesame seeds before serving.

Nutritional Values: Calories: 301 kcal Carbohydrates: 14g Protein: 30g Fat: 14g

Saturated Fat: 4g Cholesterol: 69mg Sodium: 715mg Potassium: 782mg Fiber: 4g Sugar: 6g Vitamin A: 118% DV Vitamin C: 79% DV Calcium: 7% DV Iron: 20% DV

Quinoa and vegetable salad with lemon vinaigrette

Preparation time: 20 minutes **Cooking Time:** 20 minutes (for quinoa) **Servings:** 4 **Difficulty:** Easy

Ingredients:

For the salad:

- 1 cup quinoa
- 2 cups water
- 1/2 cup chopped cucumber.
- 1/2 cup chopped bell pepper.
- 1/2 cup chopped carrot.
- 1/4 cup chopped scallions (green part only)
- 1/4 cup chopped fresh parsley.
- 1/4 cup chopped fresh cilantro.
- 1/4 cup chopped walnuts.
- Salt and pepper to taste

For the dressing:

- 1/4 cup olive oil
- 2 tablespoons fresh lemon juice
- 1 teaspoon Dijon mustard
- 1 teaspoon maple syrup
- Salt and pepper to taste

Instructions:

1. Rinse the quinoa in cold water and drain. Bring the water to a boil in a saucepan, add the quinoa, and reduce the heat to low. Cover and simmer for 15-20 minutes or until the water is absorbed and the quinoa is tender. Fluff with a fork and let cool.
2. Combine the cooled quinoa, cucumber, bell pepper, carrot, scallions, parsley, cilantro, and walnuts in a large mixing bowl. Season with salt and pepper to taste.
3. Whisk together the olive oil, lemon juice, Dijon mustard, and maple syrup to make the dressing in a small bowl. Season with salt and pepper to taste.
4. Drizzle the dressing over the quinoa salad and toss to combine.
5. Serve chilled or at room temperature.

Nutritional Values: Calories: 330 kcal Fat: 23g Carbohydrates: 26g Fiber: 5g Protein: 6g Sodium: 50mg

63.Turkey And Avocado Sandwich with Bread

Preparation time: 10 minutes **Cooking Time:** None **Servings:** 1 **Difficulty:** Easy
Ingredients:

- 2 slices of gluten-free bread
- 2-3 oz sliced turkey breast
- 1/2 avocado, sliced.
- 1 small handful of lettuce
- 1 small handful of spinach
- 1 tbsp mayonnaise (low FODMAP)
- 1 tsp Dijon mustard (low FODMAP)
- Salt and pepper to taste

Instructions:

1. Toast the slices of gluten-free bread until golden brown.
2. In a small bowl, mix the low-FODMAP mayonnaise and Dijon mustard. Season with salt and pepper to taste.
3. Spread the mixture onto one side of each slice of toast.
4. Layer the sliced turkey breast, avocado slices, lettuce, and spinach onto one slice of bread.
5. Top with the other piece of bread, with the spread side facing down.
6. Serve immediately.

Nutritional Values: Calories: 390 kcal Carbohydrates: 26 g Protein: 18 g Fat: 24 g Saturated Fat: 3.5 g Fiber: 6 g Sodium: 500 mg

64. Shrimp And Quinoa Bowl with Roasted Vegetables and Gluten-Free Dressing

Preparation time: 15 minutes **Cooking Time:** 30 minutes **Servings:** 4 **Difficulty:** Easy

Ingredients: For the bowl:

- 1 cup quinoa, rinsed.
- 2 cups water
- 1 lb. shrimp peeled and deveined.
- 2 red bell peppers, sliced.
- 2 zucchinis, sliced.
- 2 tbsp. olive oil
- Salt and pepper, to taste
- 4 cups mixed greens
- 1/4 cup chopped fresh parsley.
- 1/4 cup chopped fresh cilantro.

For the dressing:

- 1/4 cup olive oil
- 2 tbsp. white wine vinegar
- 2 tbsp. lemon juice
- 1 tbsp. Dijon mustard
- 1 tsp. maple syrup
- Salt and pepper, to taste

Instructions:

1. Preheat oven to 400°F. Line a baking sheet with parchment paper.
2. In a medium pot, combine quinoa and water. Bring to a boil, then reduce heat to low and simmer for 20 minutes or until the quinoa is cooked and the water has been absorbed. Fluff with a fork and set aside.
3. Meanwhile, in a bowl, combine shrimp, red bell peppers, zucchini, olive oil, salt,

and pepper. Toss until coated. Arrange in a single layer on the prepared baking sheet. Roast for 10-12 minutes, or until the shrimp is pink and cooked and the vegetables are tender.
4. In a small bowl, whisk together all dressing ingredients.
5. To assemble the bowls, divide the mixed greens among 4 bowls. Top with quinoa and roasted shrimp and vegetables. Drizzle with dressing and sprinkle with parsley and cilantro.

Nutritional Values: Calories: 465kcal Fat: 21g Saturated fat: 3g Cholesterol: 214mg Sodium: 315mg Potassium: 944mg Carbohydrates: 37g Fiber: 7g Sugar: 7g Protein: 34g Vitamin A: 3267IU Vitamin C: 132mg Calcium: 176mg Iron: 5mg

Vegetable and black bean tacos with avocado cream.

Preparation time: 15 minutes **Cooking Time:** 20 minutes **Servings:** 4 **Difficulty:** Easy

Ingredients:

For the tacos:

- 1 tablespoon olive oil
- 1 red bell pepper, sliced.
- 1 yellow bell pepper, sliced.
- 1 small zucchini, sliced.
- 1 small yellow squash, sliced.
- 1 can black beans, drained and rinsed.
- 1 teaspoon chili powder
- 1 teaspoon ground cumin
- Salt and pepper, to taste
- 8 gluten-free taco shells
- Fresh cilantro, chopped.

For the avocado cream:

- 1 ripe avocado pitted and peeled.
- 1/4 cup lactose-free sour cream
- 1 garlic clove, minced.
- 2 tablespoons fresh lime juice

- Salt and pepper, to taste

Instructions:

1. Preheat the oven to 350°F (180°C).
2. In a large skillet over medium heat, heat the olive oil. Add the sliced red and yellow bell peppers, zucchini, and yellow squash. Cook for about 10 minutes, stirring occasionally, until the vegetables are tender and lightly browned.
3. Add the drained and rinsed black beans, chili powder, ground cumin, salt, and pepper to the skillet. Stir until well combined and cook for an additional 5 minutes.
4. Meanwhile, place the taco shells on a baking sheet and bake in the oven for 5-7 minutes until heated through.
5. Place the pitted and peeled avocado, lactose-free sour cream, minced garlic, fresh lime juice, salt, and pepper in a blender or food processor to make the avocado cream. Blend until smooth and creamy.
6. Fill each taco shell with the vegetable and black bean mixture to assemble the tacos. Top with fresh cilantro and a dollop of avocado cream.
7. Serve hot and enjoy!

Nutritional Values: Calories: 341kcal Fat: 18g Carbohydrates: 38g Protein: 10g Fiber: 11g Sugar: 6g Sodium: 426mg

Dinner

65. Grilled Chicken with Roasted Vegetables and Quinoa

Preparation time: 10 minutes **Cooking Time:** 30 minutes **Servings:** 4 **Difficulty:** Easy
Ingredients:
- 4 boneless, skinless chicken breasts
- 1 medium zucchini, sliced.
- 1 medium yellow squash, sliced.
- 1 red bell pepper, sliced.
- 1 yellow bell pepper, sliced.
- 1 cup cherry tomatoes, halved.
- 1/4 cup olive oil
- 1 teaspoon dried oregano
- Salt and black pepper, to taste
- 1 cup uncooked quinoa
- 2 cups water
- 1 tablespoon lemon juice
- 2 tablespoons chopped fresh parsley.
- Lemon wedges for serving.

Instructions:
1. Preheat the oven to 400°F (200°C).
2. In a large bowl, combine the sliced zucchini, yellow squash, red and yellow bell peppers, cherry tomatoes, olive oil, dried oregano, salt, and black pepper. Toss to coat the vegetables evenly.
3. Arrange the vegetables in a single layer on a large baking sheet. Roast for 25-30 minutes or until the vegetables are tender and lightly browned.
4. While the vegetables are roasted, prepare the quinoa. Rinse the quinoa under cold running water and drain well. Place the quinoa and water in a medium saucepan and boil over high heat. Reduce the heat to low, cover, and simmer for 15-20 minutes or until the water is absorbed and the quinoa is tender. Fluff the quinoa with a fork and stir in the lemon juice and chopped parsley.
5. Preheat a grill or grill pan over medium-high heat. Season the chicken breasts with salt and black pepper. Grill the chicken for 5-6 minutes per side or until cooked through and no longer pink in the center.
6. To serve, divide the quinoa and roasted vegetables among four plates. Top each dish with a grilled chicken breast and a lemon wedge.

Nutritional Values: Calories: 447kcal Carbohydrates: 37g Protein: 38g Fat: 16g Saturated Fat: 2.6g Cholesterol: 86mg Sodium: 81mg Fiber: 6g Sugar: 5g

66. Spaghetti With Meat Sauce and Parmesan Cheese

Preparation time: 10 minutes **Cooking Time:** 35 minutes **Servings:** 4 **Difficulty:** Easy
Ingredients:
- 8 ounces of gluten-free spaghetti
- 1 pound ground beef
- 1 tablespoon garlic-infused oil
- 1/2 cup low FODMAP marinara sauce
- 1/4 cup chopped fresh parsley.
- Salt and pepper, to taste
- 1/4 cup grated parmesan cheese.

Instructions:
1. Cook the gluten-free spaghetti according to the package instructions until al dente. Drain and set aside.
2. Add garlic-infused oil and ground beef in a large skillet over medium-high heat.

Cook until the meat is browned, breaking it into small pieces as it cooks.

3. Stir in the marinara sauce and chopped parsley. Bring the sauce to a simmer and cook for 10-15 minutes, until the sauce has thickened slightly.

4. Season the sauce with salt and pepper to taste.

5. Divide the cooked spaghetti between four plates. Top each dish with a generous scoop of the meat sauce.

6. If desired, sprinkle each plate with grated parmesan cheese and additional chopped parsley.

Nutritional Values: Calories: 484kcal Carbohydrates: 42g Protein: 31g Fat: 21g Saturated Fat: 8g Cholesterol: 86mg Sodium: 324mg Potassium: 536mg Fiber: 2g Sugar: 2g Vitamin A: 377IU Vitamin C: 5mg Calcium: 143mg Iron: 4mg

67. Baked Salmon with Roasted Sweet Potatoes and Asparagus

Preparation time: 10 minutes **Cooking Time:** 25 minutes **Servings:** 2 **Difficulty:** Easy
Ingredients:
- 2 salmon fillets (about 6 oz each)
- 2 small, sweet potatoes, peeled and cubed.
- 1 bunch of asparagus, trimmed.
- 2 tablespoons olive oil
- 1 teaspoon dried dill
- Salt and pepper to taste

Instructions:
1. Preheat the oven to 400°F (200°C).
2. Place the sweet potato cubes on a baking sheet and drizzle with 1 tablespoon of olive oil. Season with salt and pepper and toss to coat.
3. Roast the sweet potatoes for 10 minutes.

4. Meanwhile, rub the salmon fillets with the remaining olive oil and season with dried dill, salt, and pepper.

5. After 10 minutes of roasting the sweet potatoes, remove the baking sheet from the oven and add the asparagus. Toss to coat with any remaining oil on the baking sheet.

6. Place the salmon fillets on the sweet potatoes and return the baking sheet to the oven.

7. Bake for 15 minutes or until the salmon is cooked and the sweet potatoes and asparagus are tender.

8. Serve hot and enjoy!

Nutritional Values: Calories: 450 kcal Fat: 22 g Carbohydrates: 30 g Fiber: 6 g Protein: 35 g Sodium: 120 mg

68. Turkey Meatloaf with Mashed Potatoes and Green Beans

Preparation time: 20 minutes **Cooking Time:** 1-hour **Servings:** 6-8 **Difficulty:** Easy
Ingredients:
For the meatloaf:
- 2 pounds of ground turkey
- 1/2 cup gluten-free breadcrumbs
- 2 eggs
- 1/4 cup lactose-free milk
- 1/2 cup chopped carrots.
- 1/2 cup chopped red bell pepper.
- 1/2 cup chopped zucchini.
- 1/4 cup chopped scallions (green part only)
- 2 tablespoons chopped fresh parsley.
- 1 tablespoon garlic-infused oil
- 1 tablespoon Dijon mustard
- 1 tablespoon low-FODMAP ketchup
- 1/2 teaspoon dried thyme
- Salt and pepper to taste

For the mashed potatoes:
- 2 pounds potatoes peeled and cubed.
- 1/4 cup lactose-free milk
- 2 tablespoons butter
- Salt and pepper to taste

For the green beans:
- 1-pound green beans, trimmed
- 2 tablespoons olive oil
- 2 tablespoons chopped fresh parsley.
- Salt and pepper to taste

Instructions:

1. Preheat the oven to 375°F (190°C).
2. Mix the ground turkey, gluten-free breadcrumbs, eggs, lactose-free milk, chopped carrots, red bell pepper, zucchini, scallions, chopped fresh parsley in a large bowl, garlic-infused oil, Dijon mustard, low FODMAP ketchup, dried thyme, salt, and pepper until well combined.
3. Transfer the turkey mixture to a loaf pan and smooth the top with a spatula.
4. Bake the meatloaf in the oven for 50-60 minutes or until the internal temperature reaches 165°F (74°C).
5. While the meatloaf is baking, prepare the mashed potatoes and green beans.
6. For the mashed potatoes, boil the potatoes in a pot of salted water until tender, then drain and mash with lactose-free milk, butter, salt, and pepper to taste.
7. Heat the olive oil in a pan over medium heat for the green beans. Add the green beans and cook for 5-7 minutes or until tender. Season with chopped fresh parsley, salt, and pepper to taste.
8. Once the meatloaf is done, remove it from the oven and let it rest for 5-10 minutes before slicing.
9. Serve the meatloaf with the mashed potatoes and green beans on the side.

Nutritional Values: Calories: 380 Fat: 17g Carbohydrates: 24g Fiber: 4g Protein: 33g

69. Chicken And Vegetable Curry with Brown Rice

Preparation time: 10 minutes **Cooking Time:** 30 minutes **Servings:** 4 **Difficulty:** Easy

Ingredients:

- 1 tablespoon garlic-infused oil
- 1 teaspoon grated ginger
- 1 teaspoon ground cumin
- 1 teaspoon ground coriander
- 1 teaspoon turmeric
- 1/2 teaspoon ground cinnamon
- 1/4 teaspoon cayenne pepper
- 1-pound boneless, skinless chicken breasts cut into small pieces
- 2 cups mixed vegetables (such as bell peppers, carrots, and zucchini), sliced.
- 1 can (14.5 ounces) diced tomatoes, drained.
- 1 cup low FODMAP chicken broth
- Salt and pepper, to taste
- 2 cups cooked brown rice.
- Fresh cilantro, chopped (optional)

Instructions:

1. Heat the garlic-infused oil over medium heat in a large skillet or wok. Add the ginger, cumin, coriander, turmeric, cinnamon, and cayenne pepper. Cook for 1-2 minutes, stirring frequently, until fragrant.
2. Add the chicken to the skillet and cook for 5-7 minutes, until browned on all sides.
3. Add the mixed vegetables, diced tomatoes, and chicken broth to the skillet. Bring to a boil, then reduce heat

and let simmer for 15-20 minutes, or until the vegetables are tender and the chicken is cooked.

4. Season with salt and pepper to taste.

5. Serve the curry over brown rice, and garnish with chopped cilantro, if desired.

Nutritional Values: Calories: 380kcal Carbohydrates: 41g Protein: 32g Fat: 9g Saturated Fat: 1.5g Cholesterol: 70mg Sodium: 330mg Fiber: 5g Sugar: 4g

70. Vegetable Stir-Fry with Tofu and Brown Rice

Preparation time: 15 minutes **Cooking Time:** 20 minutes **Servings:** 4 **Difficulty:** Easy
Ingredients:
- 1 cup uncooked brown rice
- 1 tablespoon olive oil
- 1 block of firm tofu, drained and cubed.
- 2 medium carrots peeled and sliced.
- 1 small red bell pepper seeded and sliced.
- 1 small zucchini, sliced.
- 1 cup green beans, trimmed.
- 1 tablespoon grated ginger
- 2 tablespoons gluten-free soy sauce
- 1 tablespoon rice vinegar
- 1 teaspoon sesame oil
- Salt and pepper to taste

Instructions:
1. Cook brown rice according to package instructions and set aside.
2. Heat olive oil in a large pan over medium-high heat. Add tofu and cook until golden brown, about 5-7 minutes. Remove tofu from the pan and set aside.
3. Add carrots, red bell pepper, zucchini, and green beans to the same pan and cook until tender, about 5-7 minutes.

4. Add grated ginger to the pan and cook for an additional minute.

5. Whisk together gluten-free soy sauce, rice vinegar, and sesame oil in a small bowl.

6. Add the cooked tofu and brown rice to the pan with the vegetables. Pour the soy sauce mixture over the top and stir to combine.

7. Cook for 2-3 minutes to allow the flavors to meld together.

8. Season with salt and pepper to taste.

9. Serve hot and enjoy!

Nutritional Values: Calories: 302kcal Fat: 10g Carbohydrates: 39g Fiber: 5g Protein: 15g

71. Stuffed Bell Peppers with Quinoa and Feta Cheese

Preparation time: 15 minutes **Cooking Time:** 35 minutes **Servings:** 4 **Difficulty:** Easy
Ingredients:
- 4 large bell peppers, tops removed, and seeds removed.
- 1 cup cooked quinoa
- 1/2 cup crumbled feta cheese
- 1/2 cup chopped spinach.
- 1/2 cup chopped tomatoes.
- 1/4 cup chopped green onions (green part only)
- 2 tablespoons olive oil
- 1 teaspoon dried oregano
- Salt and pepper to taste

Instructions:
1. Preheat the oven to 375°F.

2. Combine the cooked quinoa, feta cheese, chopped spinach, chopped tomatoes, green onions, olive oil, dried oregano, salt, and pepper in a large mixing bowl. Mix well.

3. Stuff the bell peppers with the quinoa

mixture, pressing lightly to fill each pepper to the top.

4. Place the stuffed peppers in a baking dish and bake in the oven for 30-35 minutes, until the peppers are tender, and the filling is heated.

5. Let the peppers cool for a few minutes before serving.

Nutritional Values: Calories: 215 kcal Protein: 8g Fat: 11g Carbohydrates: 22g Fiber: 5g Sugar: 7g Sodium: 340mg

Shrimp and vegetable stir-fry with gluten-free soy sauce

Preparation time: 15 minutes **Cooking Time:** 15 minutes **Servings:** 2-3 **Difficulty:** Easy

Ingredients:

- 1 lb. raw shrimp peeled and deveined.
- 1 red bell pepper, sliced.
- 1 zucchini, sliced.
- 1 carrot peeled and sliced.
- 2 tbsp garlic-infused olive oil
- 1 tbsp gluten-free soy sauce
- 1 tbsp rice vinegar
- 1 tsp sesame oil
- Salt and pepper to taste
- Green onions, sliced (optional, for garnish)

Instructions:

1. Whisk together the soy sauce, rice vinegar, sesame oil, and a pinch of salt and pepper in a small bowl. Set aside.

2. Heat the garlic-infused olive oil in a large pan over medium-high heat. Add the bell pepper, zucchini, carrot, and stir-fry for 2-3 minutes or until the vegetables are slightly softened.

3. Add the shrimp to the pan and stir-fry for another 3-4 minutes or until the shrimp are cooked.

4. Pour the soy sauce mixture over the shrimp and vegetables and stir to coat everything evenly.

5. Serve the stir-fry hot, garnished with sliced green onions if desired.

Nutritional Values: Calories: 233 kcal Fat: 10.4 g Carbohydrates: 9.4 g Fiber: 2.6 g Protein: 25.2 g Sodium: 589 mg

72. Balsamic Glazed Pork Chops with Roasted Brussels Sprouts And Potatoes

Preparation time: 15 minutes **Cooking Time:** 45 minutes **Servings:** 4 **Difficulty:** Easy

Ingredients:

- 4 bone-in pork chops
- 2 tbsp olive oil
- Salt and pepper to taste
- 1/4 cup balsamic vinegar
- 2 tbsp maple syrup
- 1 tbsp Dijon mustard
- 1 tsp minced garlic
- 1 lb. Brussels sprouts trimmed and halved.
- 1 lb. baby potatoes, halved.
- 2 tbsp chopped fresh rosemary.

Instructions:

1. Preheat the oven to 400°F (200°C).

2. Season the pork chops with salt and pepper.

3. Heat 1 tbsp of olive oil in a large skillet over medium-high heat. Add the pork chops and cook for 3-4 minutes per side until browned. Remove from the skillet and place on a baking sheet.

4. Whisk together the balsamic vinegar, maple syrup, Dijon mustard, and minced garlic in a small bowl.

5. Brush the pork chops with half of the balsamic glaze and place them in the oven. Bake for 15-20 minutes or until the internal temperature reaches 145°F (63°C).

6. Toss the Brussels sprouts and potatoes with olive oil, salt, pepper, and chopped rosemary in a large bowl.

7. Arrange the vegetables around the pork chops on the baking sheet and drizzle with the remaining balsamic glaze.

8. Bake for another 20-25 minutes or until the vegetables are tender and the pork chops are fully cooked.

9. Let the pork chops rest for 5 minutes before serving.

Nutritional Values: Calories: 490 kcal Fat: 22g Carbohydrates: 38g Fiber: 7g Protein: 38g

73. Stuffed Chicken Breasts with Spinach and Feta Cheese

Preparation time: 20 minutes **Cooking Time:** 35 minutes **Servings:** 4 **Difficulty:** Medium
Ingredients:

- 4 boneless, skinless chicken breasts
- 2 cups baby spinach, chopped.
- 1/2 cup crumbled feta cheese
- 1/4 cup chopped sun-dried tomatoes (oil-packed)
- 2 tablespoons chopped fresh basil.
- 2 tablespoons chopped fresh parsley.
- 1 tablespoon olive oil
- 1 teaspoon garlic powder
- Salt and pepper
- Toothpicks
- 1 cup gluten-free breadcrumbs
- 1/4 cup grated Parmesan cheese.
- 2 tablespoons melted butter.

Instructions:

1. Preheat the oven to 375°F (190°C).

2. Combine chopped spinach, feta cheese, sun-dried tomatoes, basil, parsley, garlic powder, salt, and pepper in a mixing bowl. Mix well.

3. With a sharp knife, butterfly the chicken breasts by slicing horizontally through the thickest part of each breast.

4. Spoon the spinach and feta mixture onto one side of each chicken breast, leaving a border of about 1/2 inch.

5. Fold the other side of the chicken breast over the filling and secure the edges with toothpicks.

6. Combine gluten-free breadcrumbs, Parmesan cheese, and melted butter in a separate mixing bowl. Mix well.

7. Coat the stuffed chicken breasts with the breadcrumb mixture.

8. Heat olive oil in a large skillet over medium-high heat.

9. Add the stuffed chicken breasts to the skillet and cook until browned on all sides, about 3-4 minutes per side.

10. Transfer the chicken breasts to a baking dish and bake in the preheated oven for 20-25 minutes or until the internal temperature of the chicken reaches 165°F (74°C).

11. Remove the toothpicks before serving.

Nutritional Values: Calories: 370 Protein: 44g Fat: 14g Carbohydrates: 13g Fiber: 2g Sugar: 2g Sodium: 750mg

74. Steak And Roasted Vegetable Kebabs with Gluten-Free Teriyaki Sauce

Preparation time: 20 minutes **Cooking Time:** 20 minutes **Servings:** 4 **Difficulty:** Easy
Ingredients:

- 1 lb. sirloin steak, cut into 1-inch cubes.
- 1 red bell pepper, cut into 1-inch pieces.
- 1 green bell pepper, cut into 1-inch pieces.
- 1 zucchini, sliced into rounds.
- 1 red onion, cut into 1-inch pieces.
- 8 skewers
- 1/2 cup gluten-free tamari sauce
- 1/4 cup rice vinegar
- 2 tbsp. maple syrup
- 1 tbsp. grated fresh ginger.
- 2 garlic cloves, minced.
- 1 tbsp. cornstarch
- 1 tbsp. water
- Salt and pepper to taste
- Cooking spray

Instructions:

1. Preheat the grill to medium-high heat.
2. Thread steak, bell peppers, zucchini, and red onion onto skewers.
3. Whisk together tamari sauce, rice vinegar, maple syrup, ginger, and garlic in a small saucepan. Bring to a boil, then reduce heat and simmer for 5 minutes.
4. In a small bowl, whisk together cornstarch and water. Add to the saucepan and whisk until thickened about 1 minute.
5. Season kebabs with salt and pepper and spray with cooking spray.
6. Place kebabs on the grill and cook for 8-10 minutes, flipping once, until steak is cooked to the desired doneness and vegetables are tender.
7. Brush teriyaki sauce over kebabs and grill for 1-2 minutes until the sauce is caramelized.
8. Serve kebabs hot with additional teriyaki sauce on the side.

Nutritional Values: Calories: 311 kcal Protein: 30 g Fat: 9 g Carbohydrates: 27 g Fiber: 4 g Sugar: 15 g Sodium: 1857 mg

75. Roasted Vegetable Lasagna with Gluten-Free Noodles

Preparation time: 20 minutes **Cooking Time:** 1-hour **Servings:** 8-10 **Difficulty:** Medium
Ingredients:

- 9 gluten-free lasagna noodles
- 2 zucchinis, sliced.
- 2 yellow squashes, sliced.
- 1 red bell pepper, sliced.
- 1 yellow onion, sliced.
- 1 cup cherry tomatoes
- 2 tablespoons olive oil
- Salt and pepper to taste
- 2 cups lactose-free ricotta cheese
- 1/2 cup chopped fresh parsley.
- 1 egg
- 2 cups low FODMAP marinara sauce
- 1 cup grated parmesan cheese.

Instructions:

1. Preheat the oven to 375°F.
2. Cook the gluten-free lasagna noodles according to the package instructions. Drain and set aside.
3. Toss the sliced zucchini, yellow squash, red bell pepper, yellow onion, and cherry tomatoes with olive oil, salt, and pepper. Place the vegetables on a baking sheet and roast in the oven for 20-25 minutes or until tender.
4. Combine the lactose-free ricotta cheese, chopped fresh parsley, and egg in a medium mixing bowl. Mix well.
5. Spread a thin layer of the low FODMAP marinara sauce on the bottom of a 9x13-inch baking dish.
6. Place 3 cooked lasagna noodles on top of the sauce.
7. Spread half of the ricotta mixture over the noodles.

8. Add half of the roasted vegetables on top of the ricotta mixture.
9. Spoon another layer of low FODMAP marinara sauce over the vegetables.
10. Repeat layers of noodles, ricotta mixture, roasted vegetables, and marinara sauce.
11. Sprinkle the grated parmesan cheese on top of the last layer of marinara sauce.
12. Cover the baking dish with aluminum foil and bake for 30 minutes.
13. Remove the foil and bake for 15 minutes or until the cheese is melted and bubbly.
14. Let the lasagna cool for a few minutes before serving.

Nutritional Values: Calories: 365 kcal Fat: 19 g Carbohydrates: 30 g Fiber: 4 g Protein: 19 g

76. Turkey Chili With Avocado and Gluten-Free Crackers

Preparation time: 15 minutes **Cooking Time:** 45 minutes **Servings:** 6 **Difficulty:** Easy
Ingredients:
- 1 tablespoon olive oil
- 1 pound ground turkey
- 1 red bell pepper, chopped.
- 1 green bell pepper, chopped.
- 1 small zucchini, chopped.
- 1 can (14.5 oz) diced tomatoes, drained.
- 1 can (15 oz) black beans, drained and rinsed.
- 1 tablespoon chili powder
- 1 teaspoon ground cumin
- 1/2 teaspoon paprika
- 1/2 teaspoon dried oregano
- Salt and pepper, to taste
- 1 avocado, diced.
- Gluten-free crackers for serving.

Instructions:

1. Heat olive oil in a large pot over medium-high heat. Add ground turkey and cook until browned, breaking it up with a wooden spoon.
2. Add chopped bell peppers and zucchini to the pot and cook for 5-7 minutes, until vegetables are tender.
3. Stir in diced tomatoes, black beans, chili powder, cumin, paprika, oregano, salt, and pepper. Bring to a simmer and cook for 30-40 minutes, until flavors are well combined, and the chili has thickened.
4. Serve hot chili, topped with diced avocado and gluten-free crackers.

Nutritional Values: Calories: 260kcal Fat: 12g Carbohydrates: 19g Fiber: 6g Protein: 21g Sodium: 420mg

77. Vegetable And Beef Stir-Fry with Sesame Sauce

Preparation time: 15 minutes **Cooking Time:** 15 minutes **Servings:** 4 **Difficulty:** Easy
Ingredients:
- 1 pound beef sirloin thinly sliced.
- 2 tablespoons garlic-infused oil
- 2 tablespoons gluten-free soy sauce
- 2 tablespoons sesame oil
- 1 tablespoon rice vinegar
- 1 tablespoon brown sugar
- 1 teaspoon cornstarch
- 1 teaspoon grated fresh ginger.
- 1/2 teaspoon black pepper
- 1 red bell pepper thinly sliced.
- 1 green bell pepper thinly sliced.
- 1 zucchini, sliced.
- 1 cup sliced carrots.
- 1 cup chopped book choy.
- 1/4 cup chopped scallions.
- 2 tablespoons sesame seeds
- Cooked brown rice for serving.

Instructions:

1. Whisk together the garlic-infused oil, gluten-free soy sauce, sesame oil, rice vinegar, brown sugar, cornstarch, grated fresh ginger, and black pepper in a small bowl. Set aside.

2. Heat a large wok or skillet over high heat. Add the sliced beef and cook until browned about 3-4 minutes. Remove the meat from the pan and set aside.

3. Add the sliced bell peppers, zucchini, and carrots to the pan and cook for 2-3 minutes, until slightly softened.

4. Add the bok choy and scallions to the pan and cook for 1-2 minutes until the bok choy is wilted.

5. Add the cooked beef back to the pan and pour the sesame sauce over the top. Toss to coat everything evenly.

6. Sprinkle sesame seeds over the top of the stir-fry.

7. Serve the stir-fried hot cooked brown rice.

Nutritional Values: Calories: 358 kcal Fat: 22 g Carbohydrates: 18 g Fiber: 4 g Protein: 23 g

78. Baked Chicken Parmesan with Gluten-Free Breadcrumbs

Preparation time: 15 minutes **Cooking Time:** 30 minutes **Servings:** 4 **Difficulty:** Easy
Ingredients:

- 4 boneless, skinless chicken breasts
- 1 cup gluten-free breadcrumbs
- 1/4 cup grated Parmesan cheese.
- 1 teaspoon dried basil
- 1 teaspoon dried oregano
- 1/2 teaspoon garlic powder
- 1/4 teaspoon salt
- 1/4 teaspoon black pepper
- 1 egg

- 1/2 cup low FODMAP marinara sauce
- 1/2 cup shredded mozzarella cheese

Instructions:

1. Preheat the oven to 375°F.
2. Mix the gluten-free breadcrumbs, Parmesan cheese, basil, oregano, garlic powder, salt, and black pepper in a shallow bowl.
3. In another shallow bowl, beat the egg.
4. Dip each chicken breast in the egg, then coat in the breadcrumb mixture.
5. Place the chicken breasts in a baking dish and bake for 25 minutes.
6. Remove the dish from the oven and spoon the marinara sauce over the chicken breasts.
7. Sprinkle the shredded mozzarella cheese on top of the chicken breasts.
8. Return the dish to the oven and bake for 5 minutes or until the cheese is melted and bubbly.
9. Serve with your favorite low-FODMAP side dish.

Nutritional Values: Calories: 351 kcal Fat: 9 g Carbohydrates: 20 g Fiber: 2 g Protein: 47 g

79. Vegetable And Chicken Stir-Fry with Brown Rice

Preparation time: 15 minutes **Cooking Time:** 20 minutes **Servings:** 4 **Difficulty:** Easy
Ingredients:

- 2 boneless, skinless chicken breasts sliced into thin strips.
- 1 red bell pepper, sliced into thin strips.
- 1 yellow bell pepper, sliced into thin strips.
- 1 zucchini, sliced into thin rounds.
- 1 small carrot, sliced into thin rounds.
- 1/2 cup of green beans, trimmed.
- 2 tbsp garlic-infused oil

- 1 tbsp grated ginger
- 2 tbsp gluten-free soy sauce
- 1 tsp sesame oil
- 1 tbsp cornstarch
- Salt and pepper, to taste
- 2 cups cooked brown rice.

Instructions:

1. Preheat a large skillet over medium-high heat. Add the garlic-infused oil and heat for 1 minute.

2. Add the sliced chicken and cook until lightly browned about 5 minutes.

3. Add the sliced bell peppers, zucchini, carrot, and green beans to the skillet. Stir-fry for 3-4 minutes until the vegetables are tender-crisp.

4. Whisk together the gluten-free soy sauce, sesame oil, and cornstarch until smooth in a small bowl.

5. Pour the soy sauce mixture over the vegetables and chicken, stirring constantly until the sauce has thickened and evenly coated the stir-fry.

6. Season with salt and pepper to taste.

7. Serve the stir-fry hot with cooked brown rice.

Nutritional Values: Calories: 315 kcal Protein: 24g Fat: 10g Carbohydrates: 33g Fiber: 5g Sugar: 4g

80. Beef And Vegetable Stew with Gluten-Free Dumplings

Preparation time: 20 minutes **Cooking Time:** 2 hours **Servings:** 6-8 **Difficulty:** Intermediate

Ingredients:

- 2 pounds stew beef, cut into 1-inch cubes.
- 2 tablespoons olive oil
- 3 medium carrots peeled and chopped.
- 3 celery stalks, chopped.
- 1 large parsnip peeled and chopped.
- 1 small turnip peeled and chopped.

- 1 small zucchini, chopped.
- 1 small yellow squash, chopped.
- 1 cup canned diced tomatoes.
- 2 cups low FODMAP beef broth
- 1 tablespoon fresh thyme leaves
- 1 tablespoon fresh rosemary leaves
- Salt and pepper, to taste
- Gluten-free flour for dusting
- 1/2 cup gluten-free biscuit mix
- 1/4 cup lactose-free milk
- 2 tablespoons butter
- 1 tablespoon fresh parsley, chopped.

Instructions:

1. Preheat the oven to 350°F.

2. Heat the olive oil over medium-high heat in a large Dutch oven or oven-safe pot. Add the stew beef and cook until browned on all sides, about 5-7 minutes.

3. Add the chopped carrots, celery, parsnip, turnip, zucchini, and yellow squash to the pot. Cook for 5-7 minutes or until the vegetables begin to soften.

4. Add the canned diced tomatoes, beef broth, thyme, rosemary, salt, and pepper to the pot. Stir well to combine.

5. Bring the stew to a simmer, cover the pot, and transfer it to the oven. Bake for 1 1/2 to 2 hours or until the beef is tender.

6. While the stew is cooking, prepare the gluten-free dumplings. In a medium bowl, combine the gluten-free biscuit mix and lactose-free milk. Stir until a soft dough forms.

7. Dust a clean work surface with gluten-free flour. Roll the dough into small balls about the size of a ping-pong ball.

8. After cooking the stew for 1 1/2 to 2 hours, remove the pot from the oven and place it on the stovetop. Add the

dumplings to the hash, spacing them evenly on top. Cover the pot and return it to the range.

9. Bake the stew for 20-25 minutes or until the dumplings are cooked.

10. Remove the pot from the oven and stir in the butter and chopped parsley. Serve hot.

Nutritional Values: Calories: 348 Fat: 15g Carbohydrates: 16g Protein: 36g Fiber: 3g Sodium: 371mg

81.Zucchini Noodles with Turkey Meatballs and Tomato Sauce

Preparation time: 20 minutes **Cooking Time:** 35 minutes **Servings:** 4 **Difficulty:** Medium
Ingredients:
- 4 medium zucchinis, spiralized
- 1 pound ground turkey
- 1/4 cup gluten-free breadcrumbs
- 1/4 cup grated Parmesan cheese.
- 2 tablespoons chopped fresh parsley.
- 1 egg, lightly beaten.
- 2 tablespoons olive oil
- 1/2 cup diced carrots.
- 1/2 cup diced red bell pepper.
- 1/2 cup diced yellow onion.
- 1 tablespoon minced garlic
- 1 (14.5-ounce) can have diced tomatoes, drained
- 1/2 teaspoon dried basil
- 1/2 teaspoon dried oregano
- 1/4 teaspoon salt
- 1/8 teaspoon black pepper

Instructions:
1. Preheat the oven to 375°F.
2. Mix the ground turkey, breadcrumbs, Parmesan cheese, parsley, egg, 1 tablespoon of olive oil, salt, and black pepper in a large bowl. Form the mixture into 16 meatballs.

3. Heat the remaining tablespoon of olive oil over medium-high heat in a large ovenproof skillet. Add the meatballs and cook for 5-7 minutes, turning occasionally, until browned on all sides.

4. Remove the meatballs from the skillet and set them aside. Add the carrots, red bell pepper, onion, and garlic to the skillet and cook for 5 minutes, until softened.

5. Add the diced tomatoes, basil, oregano, salt, and black pepper to the skillet. Stir well and bring the mixture to a boil.

6. Return the meatballs to the skillet, submerging them in the tomato sauce. Cover the skillet with foil and transfer it to the oven.

7. Bake for 20 minutes until the meatballs are cooked through.

8. While the meatballs are cooking, spiralize the zucchinis and set them aside.

9. Once the meatballs are done, remove the skillet from the oven and place it on the stovetop. Remove the foil and add the zucchini noodles to the skillet. Toss well to coat the noodles in the tomato sauce.

10. Cook for 3-4 minutes until the zucchini noodles are heated through but still slightly firm.

11. Serve hot, garnished with additional Parmesan cheese, and chopped parsley if desired.

Nutritional Values: Calories: 327 kcal Fat: 18 g Carbohydrates: 15 g Fiber: 4 g Sugar: 7 g Protein: 27 g Sodium: 598 mg

82. Spinach And Feta Stuffed Pork Tenderloin with Roasted Vegetables

Preparation time: 15 minutes **Cooking Time:** 45 minutes **Difficulty:** Medium

Ingredients:

- 1 pork tenderloin (about 1 pound)
- 2 cups fresh spinach, chopped.
- 1/2 cup crumbled feta cheese
- 2 tablespoons olive oil
- 1 tablespoon chopped fresh rosemary.
- Salt and pepper, to taste
- 4 cups mixed vegetables (e.g., carrots, bell peppers, zucchini), chopped.
- 1 tablespoon garlic-infused olive oil
- 1/4 teaspoon salt
- 1/4 teaspoon black pepper

Instructions:

1. Preheat the oven to 375°F.
2. Cut a lengthwise slit down the center of the pork tenderloin, being careful not to cut through to the other side.
3. Combine the chopped spinach, crumbled feta cheese, olive oil, rosemary, salt, and pepper in a mixing bowl.
4. Stuff the mixture into the slit in the pork tenderloin.
5. Heat a large skillet over medium-high heat. Sear the pork tenderloin on all sides until browned.
6. Transfer the pork tenderloin to a baking dish and bake for 35-40 minutes or until the internal temperature reaches 145°F.
7. Meanwhile, toss the mixed vegetables with garlic-infused olive oil, salt, and pepper. Roast in a separate baking dish for 25-30 minutes, stirring occasionally, until tender.
8. Let the pork tenderloin rest for 5 minutes before slicing.
9. Serve with roasted vegetables.

Nutritional Values: Calories: 360 Fat: 18g Carbohydrates: 11g Protein: 36g Fiber: 3g

83. Teriyaki Salmon with Brown Rice and Green Beans

Preparation time: 10 minutes **Cooking Time:** 20 minutes **Servings:** 4 **Difficulty:** Easy

Ingredients:

- 4 salmon fillets, skin removed.
- 1/2 cup gluten-free soy sauce
- 1/4 cup brown sugar
- 1 tbsp grated ginger
- 2 tbsp sesame oil
- 2 tbsp rice vinegar
- 2 cloves garlic, minced.
- 2 cups cooked brown rice.
- 1 lb. green beans, trimmed.
- 1 tbsp olive oil
- Salt and pepper, to taste
- Sesame seeds, for garnish (optional)

Instructions:

1. Preheat oven to 400°F (200°C).
2. In a small bowl, whisk together soy sauce, brown sugar, ginger, sesame oil, rice vinegar, and garlic until well combined.
3. Arrange salmon fillets in a baking dish and pour the teriyaki sauce over them, coating each fillet evenly.
4. Bake in the oven for 15-20 minutes or until salmon is cooked and flakes easily with a fork.
5. While the salmon is baking, cook the brown rice according to the package instructions.
6. In a large skillet, heat olive oil over medium-high heat. Add green beans and

season with salt and pepper. Cook, stirring occasionally, for 8-10 minutes or until beans are tender but still crisp.

7. To serve, divide cooked brown rice among 4 plates. Top each with a salmon fillet and some of the teriyaki sauce from the baking dish. Add a portion of the cooked green beans on the side. Garnish with sesame seeds, if desired.

Nutritional Values: Calories: 437 kcal Fat: 19g Carbohydrates: 37g Fiber: 5g Protein: 30g

84. Turkey And Vegetable Soup with Gluten-Free Noodles

Preparation time: 10 minutes **Cooking Time:** 45 minutes **Servings:** 4-6 **Difficulty:** Easy
Ingredients:

- 1 pound ground turkey
- 1 tablespoon olive oil
- 1 medium carrot peeled and diced.
- 1 medium parsnip peeled and diced.
- 2 stalks of celery, diced.
- 1 tablespoon minced fresh ginger.
- 1 tablespoon chopped fresh garlic.
- 1/2 teaspoon dried thyme
- 1/2 teaspoon dried rosemary
- 1/2 teaspoon dried oregano
- 1/4 teaspoon black pepper
- 6 cups low FODMAP chicken broth
- 1 cup gluten-free egg noodles
- 2 cups chopped kale.
- 1 tablespoon chopped fresh parsley.

Instructions:

1. Heat the olive oil over medium-high heat in a large soup pot or Dutch oven. Add the ground turkey and cook, breaking it up with a wooden spoon, until browned and cooked through, about 8-10 minutes.

2. Add the carrot, parsnip, celery, ginger, and garlic to the pot. Cook, stirring occasionally, for 5-7 minutes or until the vegetables are tender.

3. Stir in the thyme, rosemary, oregano, and black pepper. Cook for 1-2 minutes, stirring frequently, until fragrant.

4. Pour in the chicken broth and bring to a boil. Reduce the heat to low and let the soup simmer for 15-20 minutes.

5. Add the gluten-free egg noodles and chopped kale to the pot. Simmer for 8-10 minutes or until the noodles are tender.

6. Remove the soup from the heat and stir in the chopped parsley.

7. Serve hot and enjoy!

Nutritional Values: Calories: 235 Fat: 9g Carbohydrates: 14g Fiber: 2g Protein: 23g

85. Vegetable And Shrimp Risotto with Parmesan Cheese

Preparation time: 10 minutes **Cooking Time:** 35-40 minutes **Servings:** 4 **Difficulty:** Medium
Ingredients:

- 1 pound shrimp peeled and deveined.
- 1 tablespoon olive oil
- 1 tablespoon garlic-infused oil
- 1 tablespoon butter
- 1 cup arborio rice
- 1/2 cup dry white wine
- 4 cups low FODMAP vegetable broth
- 1/2 cup grated parmesan cheese.
- 1 small zucchini, diced.
- 1 small yellow squash, diced.
- 1 red bell pepper, diced.
- Salt and pepper to taste

Instructions:

1. Heat the olive oil and garlic-infused oil over medium-high heat in a large skillet. Add the shrimp and cook for 2-3 minutes until pink. Remove from the skillet and set aside.
2. In the same skillet, melt the butter over medium heat. Add the arborio rice and stir to coat with the butter. Cook for 1-2 minutes until the rice starts to turn translucent.
3. Add the white wine and stir constantly until the wine is absorbed by the rice.
4. Add the vegetable broth, 1/2 cup at a time, stirring constantly and waiting until each addition is absorbed before adding the next.
5. Add the cooked shrimp, zucchini, yellow squash, and red bell pepper to the skillet when the rice is tender and creamy. Stir to combine.
6. Cook for 3-5 minutes until the vegetables are tender and the shrimp is heated.
7. Remove from heat and stir in the grated parmesan cheese. Season with salt and pepper to taste.
8. Serve hot and enjoy!

Nutritional Values: Calories: 442 kcal Fat: 14 g Carbohydrates: 49 g Fiber: 2 g Protein: 24 g Sodium: 844 mg

86. Beef And Broccoli Stir-Fry with Gluten-Free Soy Sauce

Preparation time: 15 minutes **Cooking Time:** 15 minutes **Servings:** 4 **Difficulty:** Easy
Ingredients:

- 1 pound flank steak sliced thinly.
- 3 cups broccoli florets
- 1 red bell pepper sliced thinly.
- 1/2 cup sliced carrots.
- 2 tablespoons garlic-infused oil
- 2 tablespoons gluten-free soy sauce
- 1 tablespoon cornstarch
- 1 tablespoon brown sugar
- 1/4 teaspoon ground ginger
- 1/4 teaspoon red pepper flakes
- 1/4 cup chopped scallions (green parts only)
- 2 cups cooked brown rice.

Instructions:

1. Heat a large skillet or wok over high heat. Add the garlic-infused oil and swirl to coat the pan.
2. Add the sliced flank steak and stir-fry until browned on all sides, about 2-3 minutes. Remove from pan and set aside.
3. Add the broccoli florets, red bell pepper, and sliced carrots to the pan and stir-fry for 2-3 minutes or until crisp-tender.
4. Whisk together the gluten-free soy sauce, cornstarch, brown sugar, ground ginger, and red pepper flakes in a small bowl. Add this sauce to the pan and stir to coat the vegetables.
5. Return the sliced flank steak to the pan and stir to combine with the vegetables and sauce. Cook for 2-3 minutes or until the sauce thickens and the beef is cooked.
6. Sprinkle the chopped scallions over the top of the stir-fry and serve immediately over cooked brown rice.

Nutritional Values: Calories: 360 kcal Protein: 27g Fat: 12g Carbohydrates: 37g Fiber: 6g Sugar: 6g Sodium: 460mg

87. Roasted Chicken with Sweet Potato and Green Beans

Preparation time: 10 minutes **Cooking Time:** 1-hour **Servings:** 4 **Difficulty:** Easy
Ingredients:
- 4 bone-in chicken thighs
- 2 medium sweet potatoes, peeled and chopped into small cubes.
- 2 cups fresh green beans, trimmed.
- 2 tablespoons olive oil
- 1 teaspoon dried thyme
- 1 teaspoon dried rosemary
- 1 teaspoon garlic-infused oil
- Salt and pepper, to taste

Instructions:
1. Preheat the oven to 375°F.
2. Place the chicken thighs in a large baking dish.
3. Add the sweet potatoes and green beans to the plate.
4. Drizzle the olive and garlic-infused oil over the chicken, sweet potatoes, and green beans.
5. Season with thyme, rosemary, salt, and pepper.
6. Toss everything together until evenly coated.
7. Cover the dish with foil and bake in the oven for 30 minutes.
8. Remove the foil and bake for another 30 minutes or until the chicken is cooked and the sweet potatoes are tender.
9. Serve hot and enjoy!

Nutritional Values: Calories: 391 kcal Fat: 22g Carbohydrates: 23g Fiber: 5g Protein: 26g

88. Baked Eggplant Parmesan with Gluten-Free Breadcrumbs

Preparation time: 30 minutes **Cooking Time:** 1-hour **Servings:** 4-6 **Difficulty:** Medium
Ingredients:
- 2 medium eggplants, sliced into 1/4-inch rounds.
- 1 cup gluten-free breadcrumbs
- 1/2 cup grated parmesan cheese.
- 2 eggs
- 1/2 teaspoon dried oregano
- 1/2 teaspoon dried basil
- 1/4 teaspoon garlic powder
- Salt and pepper to taste
- 2 cups of low FODMAP marinara sauce
- 2 cups of shredded mozzarella cheese

Instructions:
1. Preheat oven to 375°F (190°C).
2. Whisk the eggs, oregano, basil, garlic powder, salt, and pepper in a bowl.
3. In another bowl, combine the gluten-free breadcrumbs and parmesan cheese.
4. Dip each eggplant slice into the egg mixture, then into the breadcrumb mixture, pressing the breadcrumbs onto the eggplant to ensure it sticks. Repeat with all the pieces.
5. Place the coated eggplant slices onto a baking sheet lined with parchment paper.
6. Bake for 20-25 minutes, flipping halfway through, until golden brown and crispy.
7. In a 9x13-inch baking dish, spread a layer of low FODMAP marinara sauce on the bottom.
8. Add a layer of the baked eggplant slices to the sauce.

9. Sprinkle half of the shredded mozzarella cheese over the eggplant layer.
10. Repeat with another layer of marinara sauce, eggplant slices, and mozzarella cheese.
11. Cover with aluminum foil and bake for 35-40 minutes, until the cheese is melted and bubbly.
12. Remove the foil and bake for 5-10 minutes to brown the cheese on top.
13. Serve hot and enjoy!

Nutritional Values: Calories: 394 kcal Carbohydrates: 41g Protein: 24g Fat: 16g Fiber: 10g Sodium: 870mg

89. Baked Tofu with Roasted Vegetables and Quinoa

Preparation time: 10 minutes **Cooking Time:** 35 minutes **Servings:** 4 **Difficulty:** Easy
Ingredients:
- 1 block (14 oz) firm tofu
- 2 tablespoons garlic-infused olive oil
- 1 tablespoon low FODMAP soy sauce
- 1 teaspoon ground cumin
- 1 teaspoon smoked paprika.
- Salt and pepper to taste
- 1 red bell pepper, sliced.
- 1 zucchini, sliced.
- 1 yellow squash, sliced.
- 1 cup cherry tomatoes
- 1 tablespoon chopped fresh rosemary.
- 2 cups cooked quinoa.
- Lemon wedges for serving.

Instructions:
1. Preheat the oven to 375°F.
2. Drain the tofu and pat it dry with paper towels. Cut the tofu into 1-inch cubes.
3. Mix the garlic-infused olive oil, low FODMAP soy sauce, cumin, smoked paprika, salt, and pepper in a bowl. Add the tofu cubes and toss to coat.
4. Arrange the tofu cubes on a baking sheet and bake for 20 minutes.
5. Meanwhile, prepare the vegetables. Mix the red bell pepper, zucchini, yellow squash, cherry tomatoes, chopped rosemary, and a drizzle of garlic-infused olive oil in a large bowl.
6. After 20 minutes, remove the tofu from the oven and add the vegetables to the baking sheet. Toss everything together and return to the oven for another 15 minutes or until the vegetables are tender and the tofu is golden brown.
7. Serve the baked tofu and vegetables over cooked quinoa with lemon wedges on the side.

Nutritional Values: Calories: 298kcal Fat: 14g Carbohydrates: 28g Fiber: 5g Sugar: 5g Protein: 17g

90. Pork Tenderloin with Roasted Vegetables and Mashed Sweet Potatoes

Preparation time: 15 minutes **Cooking Time:** 30 minutes **Servings:** 4 **Difficulty:** Easy
Ingredients:
- 1 lb. pork tenderloin
- 1 tbsp. garlic-infused oil
- 1 tsp. dried thyme
- 1/2 tsp. paprika
- Salt and pepper to taste
- 2 medium sweet potatoes peeled and chopped.
- 1 tbsp. olive oil
- 1/4 tsp. cumin
- 1/4 tsp. ground ginger
- 1/4 tsp. cinnamon

- 1/4 tsp. salt
- 2 cups mixed vegetables (carrots, zucchini, bell pepper)
- 1 tbsp. olive oil
- Salt and pepper to taste

Instructions:

1. Preheat the oven to 375°F.
2. Season the pork tenderloin with garlic-infused oil, dried thyme, paprika, salt, and pepper.
3. Heat a large oven-safe skillet over medium-high heat. Add the pork tenderloin to the skillet and sear on all sides until browned, about 3-4 minutes per side.
4. Transfer the skillet to the preheated oven and bake for 20-25 minutes or until the pork reaches an internal temperature of 145°F.
5. While the pork is cooking, prepare the sweet potatoes. Place them in a large pot and cover with water. Bring to a boil and cook until tender, about 15 minutes. Drain the water and mash the sweet potatoes with olive oil, cumin, ground ginger, cinnamon, and salt.
6. Toss the mixed vegetables with olive oil, salt, and pepper for the roasted vegetables. Spread them on a baking sheet and roast in the oven for 15-20 minutes or until tender and lightly browned.
7. Serve the pork tenderloin with mashed sweet potatoes and roasted vegetables.

Nutritional Values: Calories: 310 kcal Protein: 27g Fat: 13g Carbohydrates: 22g Fiber: 4g Sugar: 8g

91. Beef And Vegetable Stir-Fry with Gluten-Free Hoisin Sauce

Preparation time: 15 minutes **Cooking Time:** 15 minutes **Servings:** 4 **Difficulty:** Easy

Ingredients:

- 1 pound beef sirloin thinly sliced.
- 2 tablespoons garlic-infused oil
- 1 red bell pepper, sliced.
- 1 green bell pepper, sliced.
- 1 zucchini, sliced.
- 1/2 cup green beans trimmed and halved.
- 2 tablespoons gluten-free hoisin sauce
- 2 tablespoons gluten-free soy sauce
- 1 tablespoon rice vinegar
- 1 tablespoon cornstarch
- Salt and pepper to taste
- Green onions for garnish
- Cooked brown rice for serving.

Instructions:

1. Whisk together hoisin sauce, soy sauce, rice vinegar, cornstarch, salt, and pepper in a small bowl. Set aside.
2. Heat garlic-infused oil in a large skillet or wok over medium-high heat. Add beef slices and cook until browned, about 2-3 minutes per side. Remove from the pan and set aside.
3. In the same pan, add bell peppers, zucchini, and green beans. Cook for 3-4 minutes, stirring frequently.
4. Add the cooked beef back to the pan with the vegetables. Pour the hoisin sauce mixture over the meat and vegetables and stir to coat.
5. Cook for 2-3 minutes, until the sauce thickens, and the vegetables are tender.

6. Serve with cooked brown rice and garnish with chopped green onions.

Nutritional Values: Calories: 288kcal Carbohydrates: 11g Protein: 30g Fat: 14g Saturated Fat: 4g Cholesterol: 74mg Sodium: 634mg Potassium: 718mg Fiber: 2g Sugar: 5g Vitamin A: 1099IU Vitamin C: 69mg Calcium: 37mg Iron: 3mg

92. Spaghetti Squash with Meat Sauce and Parmesan Cheese

Preparation time: 15 minutes
Cooking Time: 1 hour
Servings: 4
Difficulty: Easy
Ingredients:
- 1 spaghetti squash
- 1 pound ground beef
- 1 can (28 ounces) crushed tomatoes
- 1/2 cup water
- 2 tablespoons garlic-infused oil
- 2 teaspoons dried basil
- 2 teaspoons dried oregano
- Salt and pepper to taste
- 1/4 cup grated parmesan cheese.

Instructions:
1. Preheat oven to 375°F (190°C).
2. Cut the spaghetti squash in half lengthwise and remove the seeds.
3. Place the spaghetti squash halves, cut side down, on a baking sheet lined with parchment paper.
4. Bake the spaghetti squash in the oven for about 45 minutes or until the flesh is tender and easily pierced with a fork.
5. Heat the garlic-infused oil in a large skillet over medium-high heat while the spaghetti squash is baking.
6. Add the ground beef and cook, stirring occasionally, until browned and cooked through.
7. Add the crushed tomatoes, water, dried basil, oregano, salt, and pepper to the skillet. Stir well to combine.
8. Bring the sauce to a simmer and cook for about 10 minutes or until the sauce has thickened slightly.
9. Once the spaghetti squash is done, remove it from the oven and let it cool for a few minutes.
10. Using a fork, scrape the flesh of the spaghetti squash to create "noodles."
11. Divide the spaghetti squash "noodles" among four plates.
12. Top each plate with a generous amount of meat sauce.
13. Sprinkle the parmesan cheese over the top of each plate.
14. Serve immediately.

Nutritional Values: Calories: 300 Fat: 16g Carbohydrates: 18g Fiber: 4g Protein: 22g

93. Shrimp Scampi with Pasta

Preparation time: 15 minutes **Cooking Time:** 20 minutes **Servings:** 4 **Difficulty:** Easy
Ingredients:
- 12 oz gluten-free linguine
- 1 lb. shrimp peeled and deveined.
- 4 tbsp garlic-infused olive oil
- 4 tbsp unsalted butter
- 1/4 cup dry white wine
- 1 tbsp lemon juice
- 1/4 cup chopped fresh parsley.
- Salt and pepper to taste
- 1/4 cup grated parmesan cheese.

Instructions:
1. Cook the gluten-free linguine according

to package instructions, then drain and set aside.

2. Heat the garlic-infused olive oil and butter over medium-high heat in a large skillet.

3. Add the shrimp to the skillet and cook until pink, about 2-3 minutes per side. Remove the shrimp from the skillet and set aside.

4. Add the white wine and lemon juice to the skillet and cook for 1-2 minutes until slightly reduced.

5. Add the cooked linguine to the skillet, tossing to coat with the sauce.

6. Add the cooked shrimp back into the skillet and toss to combine.

7. Season with salt and pepper to taste.

8. Serve the shrimp scampi with chopped parsley and grated parmesan cheese on top.

Nutritional Values: Calories: 522 kcal Fat: 23 g Carbohydrates: 56 g Protein: 23 g Fiber: 2 g

94. Greek Yogurt Chicken with Roasted Vegetables and Brown Rice

Preparation time: 15 minutes **Cooking Time:** 30 minutes **Servings:** 4 **Difficulty:** Easy
Ingredients:
- 4 boneless, skinless chicken breasts
- 1 cup plain Greek yogurt.
- 1 tablespoon olive oil
- 1 tablespoon lemon juice
- 1 teaspoon dried oregano
- 1/2 teaspoon garlic powder
- Salt and pepper, to taste
- 4 cups mixed vegetables (such as zucchini, bell peppers, and eggplant), chopped.

- 1 tablespoon olive oil
- Salt and pepper, to taste
- 2 cups cooked brown rice.

Instructions:
1. Preheat the oven to 375°F (190°C).
2. Mix the Greek yogurt, olive oil, lemon juice, oregano, garlic powder, salt, and pepper in a small bowl.
3. Place the chicken breasts in a baking dish and spoon the Greek yogurt mixture over the top, ensuring they are evenly coated.
4. Bake the chicken in the oven for 25-30 minutes or until cooked.
5. While the chicken is cooking, toss the mixed vegetables with olive oil, salt, and pepper in a separate baking dish.
6. After the chicken has cooked for 10 minutes, add the vegetables to the oven and roast for the remaining 15-20 minutes or until tender and slightly browned.
7. Serve the roasted chicken and vegetables over cooked brown rice.

Nutritional Values: Calories: 380 kcal Carbohydrates: 33 g Protein: 38 g Fat: 12 g Fiber: 6 g Sugar: 6 g Sodium: 156 mg

95. Vegetable And Chicken Curry with Quinoa

Preparation time: 15 minutes **Cooking Time:** 25 minutes **Servings:** 4 **Difficulty:** Easy
Ingredients:
- 1-pound boneless, skinless chicken breast cut into bite-sized pieces
- 2 tablespoons olive oil
- 1 teaspoon ground turmeric
- 1 teaspoon ground cumin
- 1 teaspoon ground coriander
- 1/2 teaspoon ground cinnamon

- 1/2 teaspoon ground ginger
- 1/2 teaspoon salt
- 1/4 teaspoon black pepper
- 1 cup chopped carrots.
- 1 cup chopped zucchini.
- 1 cup chopped bell pepper.
- 1 cup chopped eggplant.
- 1/4 cup chopped fresh cilantro.
- 2 tablespoons freshly squeezed lemon juice.
- 1 cup cooked quinoa
- 2 cups low FODMAP chicken broth
- 1 cup canned low-FODMAP coconut milk.

Instructions:

1. Heat the olive oil over medium-high heat in a large skillet. Add the chicken and cook until browned on all sides, about 5-7 minutes.
2. Add the turmeric, cumin, coriander, cinnamon, ginger, salt, and pepper to the skillet. Stir to coat the chicken with the spices.
3. Add the chopped carrots, zucchini, bell pepper, and eggplant to the skillet. Stir to combine with the chicken and spices.
4. Pour in the low FODMAP chicken broth and canned coconut milk. Bring to a simmer and cook for 10-15 minutes or until the vegetables are tender and the chicken is cooked.
5. Stir in the chopped cilantro and lemon juice.
6. Serve over cooked quinoa.

Nutritional Values: Calories: 400 kcal Protein: 28g Fat: 21g Carbohydrates: 29g Fiber: 5g Sugar: 8g Sodium: 510mg

96. Steak And Vegetable Stir-Fry with Gluten-Free Soy Sauce

Preparation time: 10 minutes **Cooking Time:** 15 minutes **Servings:** 4 **Difficulty:** Easy
Ingredients:

- 1 pound sirloin steak thinly sliced.
- 2 tablespoons garlic-infused oil
- 2 tablespoons gluten-free soy sauce
- 2 tablespoons rice vinegar
- 1 tablespoon brown sugar
- 1 tablespoon cornstarch
- 1 red bell pepper, sliced.
- 1 green bell pepper, sliced.
- 1 cup snow peas
- 1 cup sliced carrots.
- 1 cup sliced zucchini.
- 1 tablespoon sesame oil
- 2 green onions, sliced.
- Salt and pepper to taste
- Cooked brown rice for serving.

Instructions:

1. Whisk together the garlic-infused oil, gluten-free soy sauce, rice vinegar, brown sugar, and cornstarch in a small bowl. Set aside.
2. Heat a large skillet over high heat. Add the sliced steak and cook until browned about 3-4 minutes. Remove the steak from the skillet and set aside.
3. Add sliced bell peppers, snow peas, carrots, and zucchini in the same skillet. Cook for 2-3 minutes or until slightly softened.
4. Add the cooked steak back to the skillet with the vegetables. Pour the sauce over the steak and vegetables until everything is coated. Cook for 2-3 minutes or until the sauce has thickened.

5. Remove the skillet from the heat and drizzle with sesame oil. Top with sliced green onions and season with salt and pepper to taste.

6. Serve over cooked brown rice.

Nutritional Values: Calories: 363kcal Fat: 19g Carbohydrates: 16g Fiber: 4g Sugar: 7g Protein: 32g

97. Turkey And Vegetable Stir-Fry with Gluten-Free Teriyaki Sauce

Preparation time: 15 minutes **Cooking Time:** 15 minutes **Servings:** 4 **Difficulty:** Easy

Ingredients:
- 1 pound ground turkey
- 1 tablespoon garlic-infused oil
- 1 red bell pepper, sliced.
- 1 yellow bell pepper, sliced.
- 1 cup sliced carrots.
- 1 cup sliced zucchini.
- 1 cup sliced yellow squash.
- 1/4 cup gluten-free teriyaki sauce
- 1 tablespoon cornstarch
- 2 cups cooked brown rice.
- Salt and pepper, to taste

Instructions:
1. Heat a large skillet over medium-high heat. Add garlic-infused oil and ground turkey. Cook until browned and no longer pink, breaking it into small pieces as it cooks.

2. Add sliced bell peppers, carrots, zucchini, and yellow squash to the skillet. Cook for 5-7 minutes, until the vegetables are tender.

3. Whisk together the gluten-free teriyaki sauce and cornstarch until smooth in a small bowl. Pour the sauce over the stir-

fry and stir until the vegetables are coated.

4. Cook for 2-3 minutes until the sauce thickens and the vegetables are coated.

5. Serve the stir-fry over cooked brown rice. Season with salt and pepper to taste.

Nutritional Values: Calories: 385 kcal Protein: 30 g Fat: 10 g Carbohydrates: 46 g Fiber: 5 g Sugar: 12 g Sodium: 557 mg

98. Baked Cod with Roasted Vegetables and Gluten-Free Bread Crumbs

Preparation time: 15 minutes **Cooking Time:** 25 minutes **Servings:** 4 **Difficulty:** Easy

Ingredients:
- 4 cod fillets (about 6 oz each)
- 1/2 cup gluten-free breadcrumbs
- 1/4 cup grated parmesan cheese.
- 1 tsp dried parsley
- 1/2 tsp dried basil
- 1/2 tsp dried oregano
- 1/4 tsp garlic powder
- Salt and pepper to taste
- 2 tbsp olive oil
- 1 red bell pepper, sliced.
- 1 zucchini, sliced.
- 1 yellow squash, sliced.
- 1/2 onion, sliced.
- 1/2 tsp dried thyme

Instructions:
1. Preheat oven to 400°F (200°C). Line a baking sheet with parchment paper.

2. Mix the breadcrumbs, parmesan cheese, parsley, basil, oregano, garlic powder, salt, and pepper in a small bowl.

3. Place the cod fillets on the baking sheet

and sprinkle the breadcrumb mixture on top of each fillet.

4. Bake in the oven for 15-20 minutes until the fish is cooked through and the bread crumb topping is golden brown.

5. While the fish is baking, heat the olive oil in a large skillet over medium heat. Add the sliced bell pepper, zucchini, yellow squash, onion, thyme, salt, and pepper. Cook until the vegetables are tender, about 10 minutes.

6. Serve the baked cod with the roasted vegetables on the side.

Nutritional Values: Calories: 345 kcal Fat: 16 g Carbohydrates: 12 g Fiber: 3 g Protein: 37 g

Snacks

99.Trail Mix with Gluten-Free Pretzels, Nuts, And Dark Chocolate

Preparation time: 10 minutes. **Servings:** 6
Ingredients:
- 1 cup gluten-free pretzels
- 1 cup mixed nuts (e.g., almonds, walnuts, pecans)
- 1/2 cup dark chocolate chips
- 1/4 cup unsweetened coconut flakes

Instructions:
1. Preheat the oven to 350°F (175°C).
2. Spread the pretzels and mixed nuts on a baking sheet and roast them for 5-7 minutes or until lightly toasted.
3. Remove the baking sheet from the oven and let the pretzels and nuts cool completely.
4. In a large mixing bowl, combine the roasted pretzels and nuts with the dark chocolate chips and unsweetened coconut flakes.
5. Toss the mixture until all the ingredients are well combined.
6. Store the trail mix in an airtight container for up to 2 weeks.

Nutritional Values: Calories: 261 Fat: 18g Carbohydrates: 20g Fiber: 4g Protein: 6g

100. Hard-Boiled Egg with Cucumber Slices

Preparation time: 5 minutes **Servings:** 1
Difficulty: Easy
Ingredients:
- 1 hard-boiled egg
- 1/2 cucumber, sliced.

Instructions:
1. Place the hard-boiled egg in a small bowl or container.
2. Cut the cucumber in half lengthwise, then slice it into thin rounds.
3. Arrange the cucumber slices around the egg.
4. Enjoy as a simple and nutritious low-FODMAP snack!

Nutritional Values: Calories: 100 Protein: 6g Fat: 8g Carbohydrates: 2g Fiber: 1g

101. Smoothie With Banana, Spinach, And Almond Milk

Preparation time: 5 minutes **Servings:** 1
Difficulty: Easy
Ingredients:
- 1 ripe banana
- 1 cup fresh spinach leaves
- 1 cup unsweetened almond milk
- 1 tablespoon maple syrup (optional)
- Ice cubes (optional)

Instructions:
1. Peel the banana and cut it into chunks.
2. Rinse the spinach leaves and pat them dry.
3. Add the banana, spinach, almond milk, and maple syrup (if using) to a blender.
4. Blend the ingredients until smooth and creamy.
5. If desired, add ice cubes to the blender and blend until smooth.
6. Pour the smoothie into a glass and enjoy!

Nutritional Values: Calories: 157kcal Fat: 3g Carbohydrates: 34g Fiber: 4g Sugar: 18g Protein: 3g

102. Roasted Chickpeas with Paprika and Sea Salt

Preparation time: 10 minutes **Cooking Time:** 30 minutes **Servings:** 4 **Difficulty:** Easy

Ingredients:

- 2 cans of chickpeas, drained and rinsed.
- 2 tbsp olive oil
- 1 tsp paprika
- 1/2 tsp sea salt
- Optional: other seasonings of your choice

Instructions:

1. Preheat the oven to 400°F (200°C) and line a baking sheet with parchment paper.
2. Toss the chickpeas with olive oil, paprika, and sea salt (and any additional seasonings) until evenly coated.
3. Spread the chickpeas in a single layer on the prepared baking sheet.
4. Roast in the oven for 25-30 minutes or until golden brown and crispy.
5. Serve hot or at room temperature.

Nutritional Values: Calories: 200 kcal Fat: 7g Carbohydrates: 28g Fiber: 7g Protein: 8g

103. Apple Slices with Almond Butter and Cinnamon

Preparation time: 5 minutes. **Servings:** 1 **Difficulty:** Easy

Ingredients:

- 1 medium apple, sliced.
- 1 tablespoon almond butter
- 1/2 teaspoon ground cinnamon

Instructions:

1. Wash and slice the apple into thin rounds.
2. Spread the almond butter onto each apple slice.
3. Sprinkle the ground cinnamon over the almond butter.
4. Serve immediately or store in the refrigerator for up to 1 day.

Nutritional Values: Calories: 160 Fat: 8g Carbohydrates: 22g Fiber: 5g Protein: 3g Sugar: 14g

104. Banana Oat Bars

Preparation time: 10 minutes **Cooking Time:** 20 minutes **Servings:** 9 bars **Difficulty:** Easy

Ingredients:

- 2 ripe bananas
- 1 cup gluten-free rolled oats.
- 1/4 cup almond butter
- 1/4 cup maple syrup
- 1/4 cup unsweetened shredded coconut
- 1/4 cup chopped walnuts.
- 1/4 cup dark chocolate chips (optional)
- 1 teaspoon vanilla extract
- 1/2 teaspoon ground cinnamon
- 1/4 teaspoon salt

Instructions:

1. Preheat the oven to 350°F (175°C). Grease or line an 8x8-inch baking pan with parchment paper.
2. In a mixing bowl, mash the bananas until smooth.
3. Add the almond butter, maple syrup, vanilla extract, ground cinnamon, and salt to the mashed bananas. Stir well to combine.
4. Add the gluten-free rolled oats, shredded coconut, chopped walnuts, and dark chocolate chips (if using) to the

bowl. Mix until all the ingredients are evenly incorporated.

5. Transfer the mixture to the prepared baking pan and spread it out evenly, pressing it down with the back of a spoon or your fingers.
6. Bake in the oven for 20 minutes or until the edges are golden brown.
7. Remove from the oven and let the bars cool completely in the pan.
8. Once cooled, cut into 9 bars.
9. Store in an airtight container at room temperature for up to 5 days.

Nutritional Values: Calories: 178 Fat: 9g Carbohydrates: 22g Fiber: 3g Protein: 4g Sugar: 9g

105. Homemade Popcorn with Olive Oil and Rosemary

Preparation time: 5 minutes **Cooking Time:** 5-7 minutes **Servings:** 2-3 **Difficulty:** Easy
Ingredients:
- 1/2 cup popcorn kernels
- 2 tablespoons olive oil
- 1 tablespoon dried rosemary
- Salt, to taste

Instructions:
1. In a large pot, heat the olive oil over medium heat.
2. Add the popcorn kernels to the pot and stir to coat them evenly with the oil.
3. Cover the pot with a lid and wait for the kernels to start popping. Shake the jar occasionally to prevent the seeds from burning.
4. When the popping slows down, remove the pot from the heat and keep it covered for another 30 seconds to allow any remaining kernels to pop.

5. Transfer the popcorn to a large bowl and sprinkle with dried rosemary and salt to taste. Toss to combine.

Nutritional Values: Calories: 150 Fat: 10g Carbohydrates: 14g Protein: 2g Fiber: 3g

106. Avocado And Tomato on Gluten-Free Toast

Preparation time: 5 minutes **Cooking Time:** None **Servings:** 1 **Difficulty:** Easy
Ingredients:
- 2 slices of gluten-free bread
- 1 small ripe avocado
- 1 small tomato
- Salt and pepper to taste

Instructions:
1. Toast two slices of gluten-free bread until they are crispy.
2. Cut a small ripe avocado in half and remove the pit. Use a spoon to scoop out the flesh into a small bowl.
3. Mash the avocado with a fork until it is smooth and spreadable.
4. Cut a small tomato into thin slices.
5. Spread the mashed avocado onto each piece of toasted bread.
6. Arrange the tomato slices on top of the avocado.
7. Season with salt and pepper to taste.
8. Serve and enjoy!

Nutritional Values: Calories: 280kcal Fat: 18g Carbohydrates: 27g Fiber: 9g Protein: 6g

107. Tuna And Gluten-Free Crackers

Preparation time: 5 minutes **Cooking Time:** N/A **Servings:** 2 **Difficulty:** Easy
Ingredients:
- 1 can of tuna, drained

- 1 tablespoon of mayonnaise (check for no high-FODMAP ingredients)
- 1 tablespoon of chopped green onion (green part only)
- 1 teaspoon of lemon juice
- Salt and pepper to taste
- Gluten-free crackers

Instructions:

1. Mix the drained tuna, mayonnaise, chopped green onion, and lemon juice in a small bowl.
2. Add salt and pepper to taste.
3. Serve with gluten-free crackers.

Nutritional Values: Calories: 161 kcal Fat: 8.5 g Carbohydrates: 5.5 g Fiber: 0.5 g Protein: 16.5 g

Carrot sticks with hummus

Preparation time: 10 minutes **Cooking Time:** None **Servings:** 2 **Difficulty:** Easy

Ingredients:

- 4 large carrots, peeled and cut into sticks.
- 1/2 cup gluten-free hummus
- 1 tablespoon extra-virgin olive oil
- Salt and pepper to taste

Instructions:

1. Wash and peel the carrots, then cut them into sticks.
2. Mix the hummus, olive oil, salt, and pepper in a small bowl until well combined.
3. Serve the carrot sticks with the hummus mixture on the side for dipping.

Nutritional Values: Calories: 165 Fat: 11g Carbohydrates: 15g Fiber: 6g Protein: 4g

108.   Granola Bars

Preparation time: 15 minutes **Cooking Time:** 20 minutes **Servings:** 12 **Difficulty:** Easy

Ingredients:

- 1 1/2 cups gluten-free rolled oats.
- 1/4 cup chopped walnuts.
- 1/4 cup sunflower seeds
- 1/4 cup pumpkin seeds
- 1/4 cup unsweetened shredded coconut
- 1/4 cup maple syrup
- 1/4 cup melted coconut oil.
- 1/4 cup almond butter
- 1/2 teaspoon cinnamon
- 1/2 teaspoon vanilla extract
- 1/4 teaspoon salt
- 1/4 cup dried cranberries

Instructions:

1. Preheat the oven to 350°F (175°C) and line an 8-inch square baking pan with parchment paper.
2. Combine the gluten-free rolled oats, chopped walnuts, sunflower seeds, pumpkin seeds, and unsweetened shredded coconut in a large mixing bowl.
3. In a separate mixing bowl, whisk together the maple syrup, melted coconut oil, almond butter, cinnamon, vanilla extract, and salt until well combined.
4. Pour the wet ingredients over the dry ingredients and stir until everything is evenly coated.
5. Fold in the dried cranberries.
6. Pour the mixture into the prepared baking pan and press it down evenly with a spatula.
7. Bake for 20-25 minutes or until the edges are golden brown.
8. Let the granola bars cool in the pan for 10-15 minutes, then use the parchment paper to lift them out of the pan and transfer them to a wire rack to cool completely.

9. Once cool, slice into 12 bars and serve.

Nutritional Values: Calories: 210 kcal Fat: 14g Carbohydrates: 18g Fiber: 3g Protein: 4g

109. Yogurt With Gluten-Free Granola and Berries

Preparation time: 5 minutes **Servings:** 1
Difficulty: Easy
Ingredients:

- 1 cup lactose-free or low-FODMAP yogurt
- 1/2 cup gluten-free granola
- 1/2 cup mixed berries (e.g., strawberries, blueberries, raspberries)

Instructions:

1. In a bowl, add the lactose-free or low-FODMAP yogurt.
2. Sprinkle the gluten-free granola on top of the yogurt.
3. Add the mixed berries on top of the granola.
4. Serve immediately.

Nutritional Values: Calories: 320 Fat: 11g Carbohydrates: 46g Fiber: 5g Protein: 13g

110. Rice Cakes With Almond Butter and Banana

Preparation time: 5 minutes **Servings:** 2
Difficulty: Easy
Ingredients:

- 2 rice cakes (make sure they are low FODMAP certified)
- 2 tbsp almond butter
- 1 banana, sliced.
- Cinnamon (optional)

Instructions:

1. Toast the rice cakes to your desired level of crispness.

2. Spread 1 tablespoon of almond butter onto each rice cake.
3. Top each rice cake with banana slices.
4. Sprinkle cinnamon on top, if desired.

Nutritional Values: Calories: 190 Protein: 5g Fat: 10g Carbohydrates: 23g Fiber: 3g Sugar: 7g

111. Protein Balls with Peanut Butter and Chia Seeds

Preparation time: 10 minutes **Cooking Time:** No cooking required **Servings:** 12 balls
Difficulty: Easy
Ingredients:

- 1 cup gluten-free oats
- 1/2 cup smooth peanut butter (unsweetened)
- 1/4 cup maple syrup
- 1/4 cup chia seeds
- 1/4 cup unsweetened shredded coconut
- 1 teaspoon vanilla extract
- A pinch of sea salt

Instructions:

1. In a food processor, pulse the oats until they are a fine flour-like consistency.
2. Add the peanut butter, maple syrup, chia seeds, shredded coconut, vanilla extract, and sea salt to the food processor. Pulse until the mixture is well combined.
3. Use your hands to roll the mixture into 12 evenly sized balls.
4. Place the balls on a baking sheet lined with parchment paper.
5. Chill the balls in the fridge for at least 30 minutes before serving.

Nutritional Values: Calories: 140 kcal Protein: 4g Fat: 9g Carbohydrates: 13g Fiber: 3g Sugar: 4g Sodium: 30mg

112.   Oatmeal With Almond Milk and Blueberries

Preparation time: 5 minutes **Cooking Time:** 5-7 minutes **Servings:** 2 **Difficulty:** Easy
Ingredients:
- 1 cup gluten-free rolled oats.
- 2 cups almond milk
- 1/2 cup blueberries
- 1 tablespoon maple syrup (optional)
- 1/2 teaspoon cinnamon
- Pinch of salt

Instructions:
1. Bring the almond milk to a boil over medium-high heat in a medium saucepan.
2. Add the oats, blueberries, cinnamon, and salt. Stir well to combine.
3. Reduce the heat to medium-low and simmer, stirring frequently, until the oatmeal is thick and creamy, about 5-7 minutes.
4. If desired, add maple syrup to sweeten the oatmeal.
5. Serve hot and enjoy!

Nutritional Values: Calories: 236 kcal Fat: 5 g Carbohydrates: 39 g Fiber: 6 g Protein: 8 g Sodium: 164 mg

113.   Gluten-Free Trail Mix Granola Bars

Preparation time: 15 minutes **Cooking Time:** 20 minutes **Servings:** 12 bars **Difficulty:** Easy
Ingredients:
- 2 cups gluten-free oats
- 1/2 cup chopped almonds.
- 1/2 cup sunflower seeds
- 1/4 cup pumpkin seeds
- 1/4 cup chia seeds
- 1/4 cup coconut oil, melted.

- 1/4 cup maple syrup
- 1 tsp vanilla extract
- 1/2 cup chopped dried cranberries.
- 1/2 cup chopped dark chocolate.
- 1/4 tsp salt

Instructions:
1. Preheat the oven to 350°F (180°C) and line a 9-inch square baking pan with parchment paper.
2. Combine the oats, almonds, sunflower seeds, pumpkin seeds, chia seeds, and salt in a large bowl.
3. Whisk together the melted coconut oil, maple syrup, and vanilla extract in a small bowl.
4. Pour the wet ingredients over the dry ingredients and mix until well combined.
5. Stir in the dried cranberries and chopped dark chocolate.
6. Press the mixture firmly into the prepared baking pan.
7. Bake for 20-25 minutes or until the edges are golden brown.
8. Let cool completely in the pan, then use the parchment paper to lift the granola out of the pan and onto a cutting board.
9. Cut into 12 bars.

Nutritional Values: Calories: 250 kcal Fat: 16 g Carbohydrates: 24 g Fiber: 4 g Protein: 5 g Sugar: 8 g Sodium: 50 mg

114.   Energy Bites with Coconut and Dates

Preparation time: 15 minutes **Cooking Time:** None **Servings:** 12 bites **Difficulty:** Easy
Ingredients:
- 1 cup pitted dates
- 1/2 cup unsweetened shredded coconut
- 1/2 cup gluten-free rolled oats.
- 1/4 cup almond flour
- 2 tablespoons chia seeds
- 1 tablespoon coconut oil

- 1/4 teaspoon vanilla extract
- Pinch of salt

Instructions:

1. In a food processor, pulse the dates until they form a sticky paste.
2. Add the shredded coconut, rolled oats, almond flour, chia seeds, coconut oil, vanilla extract, and salt to the food processor. Pulse until the mixture is well combined, and the ingredients are evenly distributed.
3. Scoop the mixture into 1-inch balls and place them on a parchment-lined baking sheet.
4. Refrigerate the energy bites for at least 30 minutes before serving.
5. Store any remaining energy bites in an airtight container in the refrigerator for up to a week.

Nutritional Values: Calories: 103 kcal Protein: 1.7 g Fat: 4.8 g Carbohydrates: 15.4 g Fiber: 2.9 g Sugar: 10.1 g Sodium: 14 mg

115. Zucchini And Cheddar Muffins

Preparation time: 15 minutes **Cooking Time:** 20 minutes **Servings:** 12 muffins **Difficulty:** Easy

Ingredients:

- 2 cups gluten-free all-purpose flour
- 1 tbsp baking powder
- 1/2 tsp salt
- 1/4 tsp black pepper
- 1 cup shredded zucchini
- 1 cup shredded cheddar cheese
- 1/4 cup chopped scallions (green parts only)
- 2 eggs
- 1/2 cup lactose-free milk
- 1/4 cup olive oil

Instructions:

1. Preheat the oven to 375°F (190°C) and line a muffin tin with 12 paper liners.
2. Whisk together the flour, baking powder, salt, and black pepper in a large bowl.
3. Stir in the shredded zucchini, cheddar cheese, and scallions.
4. In a separate bowl, beat the eggs, lactose-free milk, and olive oil together.
5. Pour the wet ingredients into the dry ingredients and stir until just combined.
6. Spoon the batter into the prepared muffin tin, filling each cup about 2/3 full.
7. Bake for 18-20 minutes until the muffins are lightly golden brown and a toothpick inserted into the center comes clean.
8. Allow the muffins to cool in the tin for 5 minutes, then transfer them to a wire rack to cool completely.

Nutritional Values: Calories: 168 kcal Fat: 9 g Carbohydrates: 17 g Fiber: 1 g Sugar: 1 g Protein: 5 g Sodium: 287 mg

116. Chocolate Chia Pudding

Preparation time: 10 minutes **Cooking Time:** None **Servings:** 2-3 **Difficulty:** Easy

Ingredients:

- 1 cup unsweetened almond milk
- 1/4 cup chia seeds
- 2 tablespoons maple syrup
- 2 tablespoons unsweetened cocoa powder
- 1/2 teaspoon vanilla extract
- Pinch of salt

Instructions:

1. Whisk together the almond milk, chia seeds, maple syrup, cocoa powder,

vanilla extract, and salt in a medium-sized bowl until well combined.

2. Cover the bowl and refrigerate for at least 4 hours or overnight until the mixture thickens and the chia seeds have absorbed the liquid.

3. Stir the mixture well before serving and divide it into serving dishes.

4. If desired, add toppings, such as fresh berries or chopped nuts.

Nutritional Values: Calories: 150 Fat: 9g Carbohydrates: 18g Fiber: 9g Protein: 5g

Salad

117.   Greek Salad with Feta Cheese, Kalamata Olives, And Mixed Greens

Preparation time: 15 minutes **Cooking Time:** 0 minutes **Servings:** 2 **Difficulty:** Easy
Ingredients:
- 4 cups mixed greens
- 1/2 cup crumbled feta cheese
- 1/2 cup pitted kalamata olives
- 1/2 cup sliced cucumber.
- 1/2 cup halved cherry tomatoes.
- 1/4 cup sliced red onion.
- 1/4 cup olive oil
- 2 tablespoons red wine vinegar
- 1 teaspoon dried oregano
- Salt and pepper to taste

Instructions:
1. Add mixed greens, feta cheese, kalamata olives, sliced cucumber, cherry tomatoes, and sliced red onion in a large bowl.
2. Whisk together the olive oil, red wine vinegar, dried oregano, salt, and pepper in a separate small bowl.
3. Drizzle the dressing over the salad and toss to combine.
4. Serve and enjoy!

Nutritional Values: Calories: 334 kcal Fat: 31g Carbohydrates: 9g Fiber: 3g Protein: 7g

118.   Chicken And Spinach Salad with Strawberries and Gluten-Free Croutons

Preparation time: 20 minutes **Cooking Time:** 10 minutes (for chicken) **Servings:** 2 **Difficulty:** Easy

Ingredients:
- 2 boneless, skinless chicken breasts
- 2 cups baby spinach
- 1 cup sliced strawberries.
- 1/4 cup gluten-free croutons
- 2 tablespoons chopped pecans.
- 2 tablespoons olive oil
- 1 tablespoon apple cider vinegar
- 1 teaspoon Dijon mustard
- Salt and pepper to taste

Instructions:
1. Preheat oven to 375°F (190°C).
2. Place chicken breasts in a baking dish and season with salt and pepper. Bake for 10-12 minutes or until cooked through. Allow the chicken to cool before slicing.
3. In a large bowl, whisk together olive oil, apple cider vinegar, Dijon mustard, salt, and pepper to make the dressing.
4. Add baby spinach, sliced strawberries, and chopped pecans to the bowl and toss with the dressing.
5. Add sliced chicken and gluten-free croutons on top of the salad.
6. Serve and enjoy!

Nutritional Values: Calories: 382kcal Fat: 24g Carbohydrates: 11g Fiber: 3g Protein: 32g Sodium: 362mg

119.   Quinoa And Mixed Vegetable Salad with Lemon Vinaigrette

Preparation time: 15 minutes **Cooking Time:** 20 minutes **Servings:** 4 **Difficulty:** Easy
Ingredients:
- 1 cup quinoa, rinsed.

- 2 cups water
- 1 red bell pepper, diced.
- 1 yellow bell pepper, diced.
- 1 small zucchini, diced.
- 1 small yellow squash, diced.
- 2 green onions thinly sliced.
- 1/4 cup fresh parsley, chopped.
- 1/4 cup fresh mint, chopped.
- 1/4 cup lemon juice
- 1/4 cup extra-virgin olive oil
- 1/2 teaspoon salt
- 1/4 teaspoon black pepper

Instructions:

1. Bring the quinoa and water to a boil in a medium saucepan. Reduce the heat to low, cover, and simmer for 18-20 minutes or until the water is absorbed and the quinoa is tender. Fluff with a fork and set aside to cool.
2. Combine the cooled quinoa, diced red and yellow bell peppers, zucchini, yellow squash, green onions, parsley, and mint in a large bowl.
3. Whisk together the lemon juice, olive oil, salt, and black pepper in a small bowl. Pour the vinaigrette over the salad and toss to combine.
4. Serve immediately, or chill in the refrigerator for at least an hour before serving.

Nutritional Values: Calories: 290 kcal Carbohydrates: 32 g Protein: 6 g Fat: 17 g Fiber: 6 g Sugar: 4 g Sodium: 300 mg

120. Tuna Salad With Mixed Greens and Crackers

Preparation time: 10 minutes **Servings:** 2 **Difficulty:** Easy
Ingredients:

- 2 cans of tuna, drained
- 1/4 cup of low FODMAP mayonnaise
- 1 tablespoon of lemon juice
- 1 teaspoon of Dijon mustard
- 1/4 cup of chopped celery
- 1/4 cup of chopped carrots
- Salt and pepper to taste
- Mixed greens
- Gluten-free crackers

Instructions:

1. Combine the drained tuna, low FODMAP mayonnaise, lemon juice, Dijon mustard, chopped celery, and chopped carrots in a mixing bowl.
2. Season with salt and pepper to taste and stir until well combined.
3. Place mixed greens onto a plate.
4. Spoon the tuna salad on top of the greens.
5. Serve with gluten-free crackers.

Nutritional Values: Calories: 289 Fat: 18g Carbohydrates: 4g Protein: 26g Fiber: 1g

121. Roasted Beet and Goat Cheese Salad with Mixed Greens And Walnuts

Preparation time: 15 minutes **Cooking Time:** 45-60 minutes **Servings:** 2-3 **Difficulty:** Easy
Ingredients:

- 3 medium beets peeled and sliced.
- 2 tablespoons olive oil
- Salt and pepper to taste
- 4 cups mixed greens
- 1/4 cup crumbled goat cheese
- 1/4 cup chopped walnuts.
- Dressing:
- 2 tablespoons olive oil
- 1 tablespoon balsamic vinegar
- 1/2 tablespoon Dijon mustard
- Salt and pepper to taste

Instructions:

1. Preheat the oven to 375°F.
2. Toss the sliced beets with olive oil, salt, and pepper, and spread them out in a single layer on a baking sheet.
3. Roast the beets for 45-60 minutes or until they are tender and caramelized.
4. While the beets are roasting, prepare the dressing. Whisk together the olive oil, balsamic vinegar, Dijon mustard, salt, and pepper in a small bowl.
5. Once the beets are done, let them cool for a few minutes.
6. Combine the mixed greens, roasted beets, crumbled goat cheese, and chopped walnuts in a large bowl.
7. Drizzle the dressing over the salad and toss to coat.
8. Serve and enjoy!

Nutritional Values: Calories: 246 kcal Fat: 21 g Carbohydrates: 10 g Fiber: 3 g Protein: 6 g

122. Chicken Caesar Salad with Gluten-Free Croutons

Preparation time: 20 minutes **Cooking Time:** 10 minutes **Servings:** 4 **Difficulty:** Easy
Ingredients:

- 1 lb. boneless, skinless chicken breasts
- 1 tsp garlic-infused olive oil
- Salt and pepper to taste
- 1 head of romaine lettuce washed and chopped.
- 1/2 cup grated Parmesan cheese.
- Gluten-free croutons
- Caesar dressing (see recipe below)

For the Caesar dressing:

- 1/2 cup mayonnaise
- 1 tbsp Dijon mustard
- 1 tsp Worcestershire sauce
- 1/2 tsp garlic-infused olive oil

- 1/4 cup freshly grated Parmesan cheese.
- Salt and pepper to taste

Instructions:

1. Preheat the oven to 400°F (200°C). Cut the chicken breasts into bite-sized pieces and place them on a baking sheet lined with parchment paper. Drizzle with garlic-infused olive oil and season with salt and pepper. Bake for 10 minutes or until cooked through.
2. Combine the chopped lettuce, Parmesan cheese, and gluten-free croutons in a large bowl.
3. To make the Caesar dressing, whisk the mayonnaise, Dijon mustard, Worcestershire sauce, garlic-infused olive oil, Parmesan cheese, salt, and pepper in a small bowl.
4. Add the cooked chicken to the salad bowl and toss with the Caesar dressing.
5. Serve the salad immediately, topped with additional Parmesan cheese and croutons if desired.

Nutritional Values: Calories: 360kcal Fat: 25g Carbohydrates: 11g Fiber: 3g Protein: 24g

123. Shrimp And Avocado Salad with Mixed Greens and Gluten-Free Dressing

Preparation time: 15 minutes **Cooking Time:** none **Servings:** 2 **Difficulty:** Easy
Ingredients:

- 6 oz cooked and peeled shrimp
- 1 ripe avocado, diced.
- 4 cups mixed greens
- 1/4 cup chopped fresh parsley.
- 1/4 cup chopped fresh chives.
- 1/4 cup gluten-free croutons
- 2 tbsp olive oil

- 2 tbsp lemon juice
- 1 tsp Dijon mustard
- Salt and pepper to taste

Instructions:

1. Combine the cooked shrimp, diced avocado, mixed greens, parsley, chives, and gluten-free croutons in a large mixing bowl.
2. Whisk the olive oil, lemon juice, Dijon mustard, salt, and pepper in a separate mixing bowl to make the dressing.
3. Pour the dressing over the shrimp and avocado mixture and toss until evenly coated.
4. Serve the salad immediately and enjoy!

Nutritional Values: Calories: 313 kcal Carbohydrates: 15g Protein: 18g Fat: 22g Fiber: 9g Sugar: 3g

124. Kale And Quinoa Salad with Cherry Tomatoes and Feta Cheese

Preparation time: 20 minutes **Cooking Time:** 20 minutes (for quinoa) **Servings:** 4 **Difficulty:** Easy

Ingredients:

- 4 cups kale, chopped.
- 1 cup quinoa, cooked.
- 1 cup cherry tomatoes, halved.
- 1/2 cup crumbled feta cheese
- 1/4 cup chopped walnuts.
- 2 tablespoons olive oil
- 2 tablespoons lemon juice
- 1 tablespoon Dijon mustard
- 1 tablespoon maple syrup
- Salt and pepper, to taste

Instructions:

1. Cook the quinoa according to package instructions and let it cool.

2. Combine the chopped kale, cherry tomatoes, crumbled feta cheese, and chopped walnuts in a large mixing bowl.
3. Whisk together the olive oil, lemon juice, Dijon mustard, maple syrup, salt, and pepper in a small bowl to make the dressing.
4. Add the cooled quinoa to the mixing bowl with the vegetables and toss to combine.
5. Drizzle the dressing over the salad and toss again to coat everything evenly.
6. Serve immediately or refrigerate until ready to serve.

Nutritional Values: Calories: 295 kcal Protein: 10g Fat: 16g Carbohydrates: 30g Fiber: 4g Sugar: 5g Sodium: 288mg

125. Roasted Chicken and Vegetable Salad with Balsamic Vinaigrette

Preparation time: 20 minutes **Cooking Time:** 30 minutes **Servings:** 4 **Difficulty:** Easy

Ingredients:

- 4 chicken thighs
- 2 cups mixed salad greens
- 1 small zucchini, sliced.
- 1 small yellow squash, sliced.
- 1 red bell pepper, sliced.
- 1 tablespoon olive oil
- 1/2 teaspoon dried thyme
- 1/2 teaspoon dried oregano
- 1/4 teaspoon salt
- 1/4 teaspoon black pepper
- 1/4 cup balsamic vinegar
- 2 tablespoons extra-virgin olive oil
- 1 teaspoon Dijon mustard
- 1 teaspoon honey

Instructions:

1. Preheat the oven to 400°F (200°C).
2. Line a baking sheet with parchment paper.
3. Season the chicken thighs on the baking sheet with thyme, oregano, salt, and black pepper.
4. Arrange the sliced zucchini, yellow squash, and red bell pepper around the chicken thighs.
5. Drizzle the olive oil over the chicken and vegetables and toss to coat.
6. Roast in the preheated oven for 25 to 30 minutes until the chicken is cooked through and the vegetables are tender.
7. Whisk the balsamic vinegar, extra-virgin olive oil, Dijon mustard, and honey to make the balsamic vinaigrette in a small bowl.
8. Divide the mixed salad greens among 4 plates.
9. Top the greens with the roasted chicken and vegetables.
10. Drizzle the balsamic vinaigrette over the top of the salad.

Nutritional Values: Calories: 300 kcal Fat: 18 g Carbohydrates: 12 g Fiber: 3 g Protein: 23 g Sodium: 270 mg

126. Spinach And Bacon Salad with Hard-Boiled Egg and Croutons

Preparation time: 15 minutes **Cooking Time:** 10 minutes (for hard-boiled eggs) **Servings:** 2 **Difficulty:** Easy

Ingredients:

- 4 cups fresh spinach
- 4 slices bacon cooked and crumbled.
- 2 hard-boiled eggs peeled and sliced.
- 1/2 cup gluten-free croutons
- 1/4 cup chopped green onions (green parts only)
- 2 tablespoons olive oil
- 2 tablespoons balsamic vinegar
- 1 teaspoon Dijon mustard
- 1/2 teaspoon maple syrup
- Salt and pepper to taste

Instructions:

1. Preheat oven to 350°F. Spread the gluten-free croutons on a baking sheet and bake for 5-7 minutes or until golden brown.
2. Combine the spinach, crumbled bacon, sliced hard-boiled eggs, and chopped green onions in a large mixing bowl.
3. Whisk together the olive oil, balsamic vinegar, Dijon mustard, maple syrup, salt, and pepper in a separate small mixing bowl.
4. Pour the dressing over the salad and toss until well combined.
5. Divide the salad between two plates and top each serving with the gluten-free croutons.

Nutritional Values: Calories: 290kcal Fat: 22g Carbohydrates: 13g Fiber: 2g Protein: 10g Shrimp and quinoa salad with mixed vegetables and dressing

Preparation time: 20 minutes **Cooking Time:** 15 minutes **Servings:** 4 **Difficulty:** Easy

Ingredients:

- 1 cup quinoa
- 2 cups water
- 1 pound shrimp peeled and deveined.
- 1 red bell pepper, diced.
- 1 yellow bell pepper, diced.
- 1 cup cherry tomatoes, halved.
- 4 green onions thinly sliced.
- 1/4 cup fresh parsley, chopped.

- 1/4 cup fresh mint, chopped.
- 1/4 cup gluten-free salad dressing
- Salt and pepper to taste
- Olive oil

Instructions:

1. Rinse the quinoa in a fine mesh strainer and place it in a medium saucepan with 2 cups of water. Bring to a boil, then reduce the heat and simmer until the quinoa is tender and the water has been absorbed for about 15 minutes. Fluff with a fork and set aside to cool.
2. Heat some olive oil over medium-high heat in a large skillet. Add the shrimp and cook for 3-4 minutes until pink and cooked. Season with salt and pepper.
3. Combine the cooked quinoa, cooked shrimp, diced bell peppers, halved cherry tomatoes, sliced green onions, chopped parsley, and chopped mint in a large bowl.
4. Drizzle the gluten-free salad dressing over the salad and toss to combine. Season with additional salt and pepper to taste.
5. Divide the salad into 4 bowls and serve immediately.

Nutritional Values: Calories: 343kcal Fat: 8g Carbohydrates: 41g Fiber: 6g Protein: 28g Sodium: 407mg

127. Greek Yogurt Chicken Salad with Gluten-Free Crackers

Preparation time: 15 minutes **Servings:** 2-3 **Difficulty:** Easy

Ingredients:

- 2 cups cooked chicken breast, shredded.
- 1/2 cup plain Greek yogurt.
- 1/2 teaspoon dried dill
- 1/2 teaspoon dried oregano
- 1/4 teaspoon salt
- 1/4 teaspoon black pepper
- 1/4 cup finely chopped cucumber.
- 1/4 cup finely chopped red bell pepper.
- 2 tablespoons chopped fresh parsley.
- Gluten-free crackers for serving.

Instructions:

1. Whisk together the Greek yogurt, dill, oregano, salt, and black pepper in a medium bowl.
2. Add the shredded chicken, cucumber, red bell pepper, and parsley. Mix well until everything is evenly coated with the yogurt dressing.
3. Serve the chicken salad immediately with gluten-free crackers.

Nutritional Values: Calories: 218 kcal Fat: 6g Carbohydrates: 5g Fiber: 1g Protein: 36g

128. Salmon And Mixed Vegetable Salad with Croutons

Preparation time: 15 minutes **Cooking Time:** 20 minutes (for salmon) **Servings:** 2 **Difficulty:** Easy

Ingredients:

- 2 salmon fillets
- Salt and pepper
- 1 tablespoon olive oil
- 2 cups mixed greens
- 1/2 cup cherry tomatoes, halved.
- 1/2 cup cucumber, sliced.
- 1/2 cup carrots, sliced.
- 1/4 cup gluten-free croutons
- 1 tablespoon fresh parsley, chopped.
- 1 tablespoon fresh dill, chopped.

For the dressing:

- 1 tablespoon Dijon mustard
- 1 tablespoon maple syrup
- 2 tablespoons olive oil
- 1 tablespoon apple cider vinegar
- Salt and pepper to taste

Instructions:

1. Preheat the oven to 375°F (190°C).
2. Season the salmon fillets with salt and pepper.
3. Heat 1 tablespoon of olive oil in a pan over medium-high heat. Sear the salmon fillets on both sides for 2-3 minutes until golden brown.
4. Transfer the salmon fillets to a baking dish and bake for 10-12 minutes until cooked.
5. Add the mixed greens, cherry tomatoes, cucumber, and carrots in a large mixing bowl.
6. Whisk together the Dijon mustard, maple syrup, olive oil, apple cider vinegar, salt, and pepper in a small mixing bowl.
7. Pour the dressing over the vegetables and toss until well combined.
8. Divide the salad between two plates and top with the baked salmon fillets.
9. Garnish with gluten-free croutons, fresh parsley, and fresh dill.

Nutritional Values: Calories: 400 kcal Carbohydrates: 18 g Protein: 29 g Fat: 24 g Fiber: 4 g Sugar: 9 g Sodium: 360 mg

129. Egg Salad With Lettuce and Bread

Preparation time: 10 minutes **Cooking Time:** 10 minutes (for boiling eggs) **Servings:** 2-3 **Difficulty:** Easy

Ingredients:

- 6 large eggs

- 1/4 cup mayonnaise (check for no high FODMAP ingredients)
- 1 tbsp Dijon mustard
- 1 tbsp chopped chives
- 1 tbsp chopped dill
- Salt and pepper to taste
- Lettuce leaves
- Gluten-free bread slices

Instructions:

1. Boil eggs: Fill a medium saucepan with enough water to cover the eggs by an inch. Bring water to a boil over high heat. Once boiling, remove from heat, cover, and let sit for 10 minutes.
2. Once boiled, drain the water, and run cold water over the eggs until they are cool enough to handle.
3. Peel the eggs and chop them into small pieces.
4. Whisk together mayonnaise, Dijon mustard, chives, dill, salt, and pepper in a mixing bowl.
5. Add the chopped eggs to the bowl and stir until well-mixed.
6. Serve on top of lettuce leaves with gluten-free bread slices.

Nutritional Values: Calories: 289 kcal Carbohydrates: 2 g Protein: 16 g Fat: 24 g Fiber: 0 g Sodium: 331 mg

130. Turkey And Spinach Salad with Cranberries and Croutons

Preparation time: 15 minutes **Cooking Time:** 10 minutes (for croutons) **Servings:** 2 **Difficulty:** Easy

Ingredients:

- 2 cups baby spinach
- 1/2-pound cooked turkey breast, sliced.

- 1/4 cup dried cranberries
- 1/4 cup walnuts, chopped.
- 1/4 cup gluten-free croutons
- 1 tablespoon olive oil
- 1 tablespoon balsamic vinegar
- 1 teaspoon Dijon mustard
- Salt and pepper, to taste

Instructions:

1. Preheat the oven to 350°F (180°C).
2. Cut gluten-free bread into small cubes to make croutons.
3. Toss the croutons in a bowl with 1 tablespoon of olive oil and a pinch of salt.
4. Spread the croutons on a baking sheet lined with parchment paper and bake for 8-10 minutes or until golden brown.
5. Whisk together the balsamic vinegar, Dijon mustard, and a pinch of salt and pepper in a large salad bowl.
6. Add the baby spinach to the bowl and toss to coat with the dressing.
7. Top the spinach with cooked turkey breast, dried cranberries, chopped walnuts, and gluten-free croutons.
8. Serve immediately.

Nutritional Values: Calories: 380 kcal Fat: 16 g Carbohydrates: 21 g Fiber: 3 g Protein: 37 g

131. Roasted Vegetable and Goat Cheese Salad with Mixed Greens And Dressing

Preparation time: 15 minutes **Cooking Time:** 25 minutes **Servings:** 4 **Difficulty:** Easy
Ingredients:

- 1 red bell pepper, sliced.
- 1 yellow bell pepper, sliced.
- 1 zucchini, sliced.
- 1 eggplant, sliced.

- 2 tablespoons olive oil
- Salt and pepper to taste
- 8 cups mixed greens
- 4 ounces goat cheese, crumbled.
- Gluten-free croutons
- For the dressing:
- 2 tablespoons olive oil
- 2 tablespoons balsamic vinegar
- 1 tablespoon Dijon mustard
- Salt and pepper to taste

Instructions:

1. Preheat oven to 400°F (200°C).
2. In a large baking dish, toss sliced bell peppers, zucchini, and eggplant with olive oil, salt, and pepper.
3. Roast in the oven for 25 minutes or until tender vegetables are lightly browned.
4. Add mixed greens, crumbled goat cheese, and gluten-free croutons in a large bowl.
5. Whisk together olive oil, balsamic vinegar, Dijon mustard, salt, and pepper in a small bowl to make the dressing.
6. Add roasted vegetables to the salad bowl and toss with the sauce. Serve immediately.

Nutritional Values: Calories: 267 kcal Fat: 21 g Carbohydrates: 15 g Fiber: 6 g Protein: 7 g

132. Tuna And Mixed Vegetable Salad with Dressing

Preparation time: 15 minutes **Cooking Time:** None **Servings:** 2-3 **Difficulty:** Easy
Ingredients:

- 2 cans of tuna (in water), drained
- 2 cups mixed greens (spinach, arugula, or lettuce)
- 1 small cucumber, sliced.

- 1 small carrot, shredded.
- 1 small bell pepper, sliced.
- 1/4 cup cherry tomatoes, halved.
- 1/4 cup black olives pitted and halved.
- 1/4 cup crumbled feta cheese
- 2 tbsp chopped fresh parsley.
- 2 tbsp gluten-free Dijon mustard
- 2 tbsp freshly squeezed lemon juice.
- 2 tbsp extra virgin olive oil
- Salt and pepper to taste

Instructions:

1. Combine the mixed greens, sliced cucumber, shredded carrot, sliced bell pepper, halved cherry tomatoes, and black olives in a large bowl.
2. Add the drained tuna to the bowl and gently mix everything together.
3. Whisk together the Dijon mustard, freshly squeezed lemon juice, extra virgin olive oil, salt, and pepper in a small bowl.
4. Pour the dressing over the salad and toss to combine.
5. Sprinkle the crumbled feta cheese and chopped parsley over the top of the salad before serving.

Nutritional Values: Calories: 255 kcal Fat: 13 g Carbohydrates: 9 g Fiber: 3 g Protein: 26 g Sodium: 820 mg

133. Mediterranean Quinoa Salad with Mixed Vegetables and Dressing

Preparation time: 15 minutes **Cooking Time:** 20 minutes **Servings:** 4 **Difficulty:** Easy

Ingredients:

- 1 cup uncooked quinoa
- 2 cups water
- 1/2 teaspoon salt
- 1/2 teaspoon black pepper
- 1 red bell pepper, diced.
- 1 yellow bell pepper, diced.
- 1 small cucumber, diced.
- 1/2 cup sliced kalamata olives.
- 1/2 cup crumbled feta cheese
- 1/4 cup chopped fresh parsley.
- 1/4 cup chopped fresh mint.
- 1/4 cup olive oil
- 2 tablespoons red wine vinegar
- 1 tablespoon Dijon mustard
- 1 tablespoon honey
- Salt and pepper to taste

Instructions:

1. Rinse the quinoa in a fine-mesh strainer and drain.
2. Combine the quinoa, water, salt, and black pepper in a medium saucepan. Bring to a boil over high heat.
3. Reduce the heat to low and cover the saucepan. Cook for 18-20 minutes or until the quinoa is tender and the water has been absorbed.
4. Remove the saucepan from the heat and let it sit for 5 minutes. Fluff the quinoa with a fork and transfer it to a large bowl to cool.
5. Once the quinoa has cooled, add the red and yellow bell peppers, cucumber, kalamata olives, feta cheese, parsley, and mint to the bowl.
6. Whisk together the olive oil, red wine vinegar, Dijon mustard, honey, salt, and pepper in a small bowl to make the dressing.
7. Pour the dressing over the quinoa mixture and toss to combine.
8. Serve the salad chilled.

Nutritional Values: Calories: 395 kcal Fat: 24 g Carbohydrates: 38 g Fiber: 6 g Protein: 10 g

134. Roasted Sweet Potato and Kale Salad with Goat Cheese And Croutons

Preparation time: 15 minutes **Cooking Time:** 30 minutes **Servings:** 4 **Difficulty:** Easy

Ingredients:

- 2 medium sweet potatoes, peeled and cut into 1-inch cubes.
- 1 tbsp olive oil
- Salt and pepper, to taste
- 6 cups kale stemmed and chopped.
- 1/2 cup gluten-free croutons
- 1/2 cup crumbled goat cheese
- 2 tbsp balsamic vinegar
- 2 tbsp olive oil
- 1 tbsp Dijon mustard
- 1 tbsp honey
- 1/4 tsp salt
- 1/4 tsp black pepper

Instructions:

1. Preheat the oven to 400°F. Line a baking sheet with parchment paper.
2. Toss the sweet potatoes with 1 tbsp olive oil, salt, and pepper in a bowl. Spread them on the baking sheet and roast for 25-30 minutes, until tender and lightly browned.
3. Massage the kale with 2 tbsp olive oil in a large bowl for 1-2 minutes until it softens.
4. Add the roasted sweet potatoes, crumbled goat cheese, and gluten-free croutons to the bowl with the kale.
5. Whisk together the balsamic vinegar, Dijon mustard, honey, salt, and pepper in a small bowl.
6. Drizzle the dressing over the salad and toss well to combine.
7. Serve immediately.

Nutritional Values: Calories: 286 kcal Protein: 7g Fat: 17g Carbohydrates: 29g Fiber: 4g Sugar: 8g Sodium: 484mg

Probiotics

135.   Kefir Smoothie with Mixed Berries and Spinach

Preparation time: 5 minutes **Servings:** 1
Difficulty: Easy
Ingredients:

- 1 cup low FODMAP kefir
- 1 cup fresh spinach
- 1/2 cup mixed berries (such as strawberries, blueberries, and raspberries)
- 1 tablespoon chia seeds
- 1 tablespoon maple syrup (optional)

Instructions:

1. In a blender, combine the kefir, spinach, mixed berries, chia seeds, and maple syrup (if using).
2. Blend on high speed until the mixture is smooth and well combined.
3. Pour the smoothie into a glass and serve immediately.

Nutritional Values: Calories: 199kcal Protein: 11g Fat: 5g Carbohydrates: 29g Fiber: 11g Sugar: 14g Sodium: 131mg

136.   Miso Soup with Tofu and Seaweed

preparation time: 10 minutes **Cooking Time:** 15 minutes **Servings:** 2 **Difficulty:** Easy
Ingredients:

- 4 cups of low-FODMAP vegetable broth
- 1/4 cup of white miso paste
- 1 tablespoon of low-FODMAP soy sauce
- 1 teaspoon of grated ginger
- 1 cup of firm tofu, cubed.
- 1/4 cup of dried seaweed, soaked in water for 5 minutes and drained.
- 2 green onions thinly sliced.
- 1 tablespoon of sesame oil
- Salt and pepper to taste

Instructions:

1. Bring the vegetable broth to a boil over medium-high heat in a large pot.
2. Reduce the heat to low and whisk in the miso paste, soy sauce, and grated ginger until the miso paste is fully dissolved.
3. Add the cubed tofu and soaked seaweed to the pot and cook for 5-7 minutes, or until the tofu is heated and the seaweed is tender.
4. Stir in the sliced green onions and sesame oil, and season with salt and pepper to taste.
5. If desired, serve the miso soup hot, garnished with additional green onions or sesame seeds.

Nutritional Values: Calories: 180 kcal Fat: 11 g Carbohydrates: 9 g Fiber: 2 g Protein: 14 g

137.   Kombucha With Fresh Ginger and Lemon

Preparation time: 10 minutes. **Servings:** 2
Difficulty: Easy
Ingredients:

- 2 bottles of unflavored low FODMAP kombucha
- 2-3 thin slices of fresh ginger
- 2 pieces of fresh lemon
- Ice cubes

Instructions:

1. Add a slice of fresh ginger and a piece

of fresh lemon to each bottle of unflavored low-FODMAP kombucha.
2. Securely close the bottles and gently shake them to mix the ingredients.
3. Refrigerate for at least 1 hour to allow the flavors to infuse.
4. When ready to serve, add ice cubes to each glass and pour the kombucha over the ice.
5. Garnish with additional ginger or lemon, if desired.

Nutritional Values: Calories: 20 Fat: 0g Carbohydrates: 4g Fiber: 0g Protein: 0g Sodium: 10mg

138. Kimchi And Tofu Stir-Fry with Brown Rice

Preparation time: 10 minutes **Cooking Time:** 20 minutes **Servings:** 4 **Difficulty:** Easy
Ingredients:
- 2 cups cooked brown rice.
- 1 tablespoon garlic-infused oil
- 1 tablespoon ginger, grated.
- 1 tablespoon soy sauce (gluten-free)
- 1 tablespoon sesame oil
- 1/2 cup kimchi, chopped.
- 1 red bell pepper, sliced.
- 1 zucchini, sliced.
- 1 package (14 oz) firm tofu, drained and cut into cubes.
- 2 green onions, sliced.
- Salt and pepper to taste

Instructions:
1. Heat the garlic-infused oil in a wok or large skillet over medium-high heat.
2. Add the grated ginger and cook for 1-2 minutes until fragrant.
3. Add the sliced red bell pepper and zucchini, and stir-fry for 3-4 minutes until tender.

4. Add the chopped kimchi, tofu cubes, and soy sauce to the wok and stir-fry for 3-4 minutes.
5. Season with salt and pepper to taste.
6. Serve the stir-fry over cooked brown rice and drizzle with sesame oil and sliced green onions.

Nutritional Values: Calories: 285 kcal Protein: 12 g Fat: 10 g Carbohydrates: 37 g Fiber: 5 g Sugar: 2 g Sodium: 271 mg

139. Sauerkraut With Roasted Chicken and Sweet Potatoes

Preparation time: 10 minutes **Cooking Time:** 45 minutes **Servings:** 4 **Difficulty:** Easy
Ingredients:
- 4 chicken thighs, bone-in, and skin-on
- 2 medium sweet potatoes peeled and chopped.
- 1 tablespoon olive oil
- 1/2 teaspoon salt
- 1/4 teaspoon black pepper
- 1/2 cup low FODMAP sauerkraut
- 1/4 cup chicken broth

Instructions:
1. Preheat oven to 400°F (200°C).
2. Toss sweet potatoes with olive oil, salt, and black pepper in a large bowl.
3. Spread sweet potatoes on a baking sheet and roast in the oven for 20 minutes.
4. While the sweet potatoes are roasting, season chicken thighs with salt and pepper.
5. Heat 1 tablespoon of olive oil over medium-high heat in a large skillet.
6. Add chicken thighs to the skillet, skin-side down, and cook for 5 minutes or until the skin is golden brown.

7. Flip the chicken over and cook for another 2-3 minutes.

8. Remove the skillet from the heat and add 1/2 cup of low FODMAP sauerkraut and 1/4 cup of chicken broth to the skillet.

9. Arrange the partially roasted sweet potatoes around the chicken in the skillet.

10. Return the skillet to the oven and roast for another 20-25 minutes, or until the chicken is cooked and the sweet potatoes are tender.

11. Serve hot.

Nutritional Values: Calories: 290kcal Total Fat: 13g Saturated Fat: 3g Cholesterol: 81mg Sodium: 459mg Total Carbohydrates: 21g Fiber: 3g Sugar: 5g Protein: 22g

140. Tempeh And Mixed Vegetable Stir-Fry with Soy Sauce

Preparation time: 15 minutes **Cooking Time:** 15 minutes **Servings:** 4 **Difficulty:** Easy
Ingredients:
- 1 package (8 oz) tempeh, cut into small cubes.
- 2 cups mixed vegetables (such as bell peppers, carrots, bok choy, and green beans), chopped.
- 2 tablespoons garlic-infused oil
- 1 tablespoon grated fresh ginger.
- 1 tablespoon gluten-free soy sauce
- 1 tablespoon rice vinegar
- 1 teaspoon sesame oil
- Salt and pepper to taste
- Cooked brown rice for serving.

Instructions:

1. Heat the garlic-infused oil in a wok or large skillet over medium-high heat. Add the cubed tempeh and stir-fry for 3-5 minutes or until lightly browned.

2. Add the mixed vegetables to the wok and stir-fry for another 5-7 minutes or until the vegetables are tender but still slightly crunchy.

3. Whisk together the gluten-free soy sauce, rice vinegar, and sesame oil in a small bowl. Pour the mixture over the vegetables and tempeh and stir well to coat.

4. Season with salt and pepper to taste. Serve the stir-fry over cooked brown rice.

Nutritional Values: Calories: 225 Fat: 11g Carbohydrates: 20g Fiber: 5g Protein: 14g

141. Pickled Carrots with Turmeric and Ginger

Preparation time: 10 minutes **Cooking Time:** 5 minutes (for boiling the vinegar mixture) Standing time: 24 hours **Servings:** 8-10 **Difficulty:** Easy
Ingredients:
- 1 pound of carrots, peeled and sliced into thin rounds.
- 1 cup of white wine vinegar
- 1 cup of water
- 1 tablespoon of salt
- 2 teaspoons of turmeric
- 1 tablespoon of grated fresh ginger
- 1 tablespoon of maple syrup
- 2 garlic cloves peeled and smashed.
- 1 bay leaf

Instructions:

1. Combine the vinegar, water, salt, turmeric, ginger, maple syrup, garlic, and bay leaf in a medium saucepan.

2. Bring the mixture to a boil over high heat, stirring occasionally.

3. Reduce the heat to low and let the mixture simmer for 5 minutes.

4. Remove the saucepan from the heat and let it cool for 10 minutes.

5. Place the sliced carrots into a large glass jar or container.

6. Pour the vinegar mixture over the carrots and stir to combine.

7. Cover the container tightly with a lid or plastic wrap.

8. Let the carrots sit in the pickling mixture for at least 24 hours.

9. Store the pickled carrots in the refrigerator for 2 weeks.

Nutritional Values: Calories: 34 kcal Fat: 0.1 g Carbohydrates: 7.8 g Fiber: 2.2 g Protein: 0.8 g Sodium: 517 mg

142. Homemade Fermented Vegetables with Dill and Garlic

Preparation time: 20 minutes Fermentation time: 5-7 days **Servings:** 8-10 **Difficulty:** Easy
Ingredients:

- 1 head green cabbage thinly sliced.
- 1 red bell pepper thinly sliced.
- 1 small cucumber thinly sliced.
- 2 carrots peeled and grated.
- 2 cloves garlic, minced.
- 2 tbsp fresh dill, chopped.
- 1 tbsp kosher salt
- 1/4 tsp black pepper
- 2 cups filtered water.

Instructions:

1. Mix the cabbage, bell pepper, cucumber, and grated carrot in a large bowl.

2. Add the minced garlic, chopped dill, kosher salt, and black pepper to the bowl. Mix everything together well.

3. Pack the mixture tightly into a large jar, pressing down firmly to release air pockets.

4. Pour filtered water over the top of the mixture, covering the vegetables thoroughly.

5. Place a weight on top of the vegetables to submerge them under water. This can be a smaller jar filled with water or a plastic bag filled with water.

6. Cover the jar with a cloth or paper towel and secure it with a rubber band. Leave the pot in a cool, dark place for 5-7 days to ferment.

7. After 5-7 days, taste the vegetables. If they fit your liking, remove the weight, and replace the cloth cover with a lid. Store the jar in the refrigerator.

Nutritional Values: Calories: 23kcal Total Fat: 0.2g Total Carbohydrates: 5.2g Dietary Fiber: 2g Protein: 1.1g

143. Homemade Coconut Yogurt with Chia Seeds and Mixed Berries

Preparation time: 10 minutes + 24 hours of fermenting **Cooking Time:** None **Servings:** 2 **Difficulty:** Easy
Ingredients:

- 1 can (13.5 oz) full-fat coconut milk
- 1 tbsp maple syrup
- 1 tbsp chia seeds
- 1/2 tsp vanilla extract
- 1/2 cup mixed berries (e.g., strawberries, blueberries, raspberries)

- Optional toppings: additional mixed berries, chopped nuts, coconut flakes.

Instructions:

1. Combine coconut milk, maple syrup, chia seeds, and vanilla extract in a blender. Blend until smooth.
2. Pour mixture into a clean jar and cover with a cheesecloth or paper towel secured with a rubber band.
3. Let the mixture ferment for 24-48 hours in a warm place (around 75-80°F) until thick and tangy. Check the mix regularly, as fermentation time may vary depending on temperature and humidity.
4. Once the yogurt is fermented, give it a good stir, and refrigerate for at least 1 hour.
5. When ready to serve, divide the yogurt into two bowls or glasses and top it with mixed berries and optional toppings.
6. Enjoy immediately or store in the fridge for up to 5 days.

Nutritional Values: Calories: 250 kcal Fat: 20g Carbohydrates: 17g Fiber: 6g Protein: 4g Sodium: 10mg

144. Probiotic Salad with Mixed Greens, Cucumber, And Kefir Dressing

Preparation time: 10 minutes **Cooking Time:** None **Servings:** 2 **Difficulty:** Easy
Ingredients:

For the salad:

- 4 cups mixed greens
- 1/2 cucumber, sliced.
- 1/2 cup cherry tomatoes, halved.
- 1/4 cup pumpkin seeds
- 1/4 cup crumbled feta cheese (optional)

For the kefir dressing:

- 1/2 cup plain kefir
- 1 tablespoon lemon juice
- 1 tablespoon chopped fresh dill.
- 1/2 teaspoon salt
- 1/4 teaspoon black pepper

Instructions:

1. In a large mixing bowl, combine mixed greens, sliced cucumber, cherry tomatoes, pumpkin seeds, and crumbled feta cheese (if using).
2. Whisk together kefir, lemon juice, chopped fresh dill, salt, and black pepper in a separate bowl until well combined.
3. Pour the kefir dressing over the salad and toss to coat evenly.
4. Serve immediately and enjoy!

Nutritional Values: Calories: 175kcal Carbohydrates: 10g Protein: 8g Fat: 12g Saturated Fat: 3g Cholesterol: 11mg Sodium: 695mg Potassium: 335mg Fiber: 3g Sugar: 5g Vitamin A: 2827IU Vitamin C: 24mg Calcium: 153mg Iron: 2mg

145. Miso-Glazed Salmon with Roasted Bok Choy

Preparation time: 10 minutes **Cooking Time:** 20 minutes **Servings:** 4 **Difficulty:** Easy
Ingredients:

- 4 salmon fillets (4-6 oz each)
- 2 tbsp miso paste
- 2 tbsp low FODMAP soy sauce
- 1 tbsp maple syrup
- 1 tbsp sesame oil
- 1 tbsp rice vinegar
- 2 cloves garlic, minced.
- 1 tbsp grated ginger
- 4 heads of baby bok choy, trimmed and halved lengthwise.

- 2 tbsp olive oil
- Salt and pepper to taste
- Sesame seeds for garnish

Instructions:

1. Preheat oven to 400°F (200°C).
2. In a small bowl, whisk together miso paste, low FODMAP soy sauce, maple syrup, sesame oil, rice vinegar, garlic, and ginger until well combined.
3. Place salmon fillets on a baking sheet lined with parchment paper. Spoon the miso glaze over the salmon, making sure to coat the top and sides of each fillet.
4. Arrange the bok choy around the salmon on the baking sheet. Drizzle with olive oil and sprinkle with salt and pepper.
5. Bake for 15-20 minutes until the salmon is cooked and the bok choy is tender.
6. Serve the salmon and bok choy hot, garnished with sesame seeds.

Nutritional Values: Calories: 355 kcal Fat: 21 g Carbohydrates: 11 g Fiber: 2 g Protein: 30 g

146. Fermented Pickles with Dill and Garlic

Preparation time: 15 minutes **Fermentation time:** 3-7 days **Servings:** 10-12 pickles **Difficulty:** Easy

Ingredients:

- 6-8 pickling cucumbers
- 1 1/2 cups water
- 1 tablespoon sea salt
- 1/4 cup white vinegar
- 2 garlic cloves, minced.
- 1 tablespoon fresh dill, chopped.
- 1/4 teaspoon mustard seeds
- 1/4 teaspoon coriander seeds
- 1/4 teaspoon black peppercorns

Instructions:

1. Rinse the cucumbers and slice them into spears or rounds. Set aside.
2. Heat the water, sea salt, and white vinegar over medium heat in a small saucepan until the salt dissolves. Remove from heat and let cool to room temperature.
3. Add garlic, dill, mustard, coriander, and black peppercorns in a quart-sized glass jar.
4. Add the cucumber slices to the jar, leaving about 1 inch of headspace.
5. Pour the brine over the cucumbers, ensuring they are entirely covered with liquid. If needed, add more water.
6. Place a lid on the jar and store it in a cool, dark place for 3-7 days, depending on how sour you like your pickles.
7. After the fermentation process, store the pickles in the refrigerator.

Nutritional Values: Calories: 11 kcal Fat: 0.1 g Carbohydrates: 2.5 g Fiber: 0.8 g Protein: 0.5 g Sodium: 296 mg

147. Probiotic Smoothie Bowl with Kefir, Banana, And Pumpkin Seeds

Preparation time: 5 minutes **Servings:** 1 **Difficulty:** Easy

Ingredients:

- 1 ripe banana, frozen
- 1/2 cup lactose-free kefir
- 1 tbsp pumpkin seeds
- 1 tbsp chia seeds
- 1/2 tsp vanilla extract

Instructions:

1. Add the frozen banana, kefir, pumpkin

seeds, chia seeds, and vanilla extract to a blender.

2. Blend on high until smooth and creamy. Add a splash of water or more kefir to reach your desired consistency.

3. Pour the smoothie into a bowl and top with additional pumpkin seeds or other toppings of your choice, such as sliced banana, coconut flakes, or nuts.

4. Enjoy immediately.

Nutritional Values: Calories: 258 kcal Fat: 8.9 g Carbohydrates: 38.1 g Fiber: 7.4 g Protein: 11.2 g Sodium: 91 mg

148. Kombucha And Green Tea Iced Tea with Fresh Mint

Preparation time: 10 minutes **Servings:** 2
Difficulty: Easy
Ingredients:

- 2 green tea bags
- 2 cups of water
- 1 cup of kombucha
- 1/4 cup of fresh mint leaves
- 2 tbsp of maple syrup (optional)
- Ice cubes

Instructions:

1. Boil 2 cups of water and steep 2 green tea bags for 5 minutes.
2. Remove the tea bags and add fresh mint leaves.
3. Let it cool for 5 minutes.
4. Strain the tea to remove the mint leaves.
5. In a pitcher, mix the green tea with 1 cup of kombucha.
6. Add 2 tbsp of maple syrup if desired.
7. Chill in the fridge for at least 30 minutes.
8. Serve over ice and garnish with fresh mint leaves.

Nutritional Values: Calories: 40 kcal Carbohydrates: 10 g Fat: 0 g Protein: 0 g Fiber: 0.5 g Sugar: 8 g Sodium: 5 mg

149. Homemade Sauerkraut with Caraway Seeds and Juniper Berries

Preparation time: 20 minutes Fermentation time: 7-10 days **Servings:** 8-10
Difficulty: Easy
Ingredients:

- 1 large head of green cabbage thinly sliced.
- 2 teaspoons kosher salt
- 1 tablespoon caraway seeds
- 1 tablespoon juniper berries
- Filtered water.
- 1-quart jar with lid

Instructions:

1. Toss the sliced cabbage with kosher salt in a large mixing bowl until well-mixed.
2. Let the cabbage sit for 10 minutes to allow the salt to absorb moisture.
3. After 10 minutes, add the caraway seeds and juniper berries to the bowl and mix well.
4. Pack the cabbage mixture into a 1-quart jar, pressing down firmly with your hands or a wooden spoon to remove any air pockets.
5. Once the jar is about 3/4 full, add enough filtered water to cover the cabbage completely.
6. Place the lid on the jar and leave it at room temperature for 7-10 days to ferment.
7. Check the sauerkraut daily, ensuring the cabbage stays submerged. If needed, add more water to cover the cabbage.

8. After 7-10 days, the sauerkraut should be ready. Taste it to ensure it is tangy and slightly sour.

9. Once the sauerkraut is to your liking, transfer it to the refrigerator to stop fermentation. It will keep for up to several months in the fridge.

Nutritional Values: Calories: 20 kcal Fat: 0g Carbohydrates: 5g Fiber: 2g Protein: 1g Sodium: 585mg

150. Coconut Water Kefir with Fresh Lime and Mint

Preparation time: 15 minutes Fermentation time: 24-48 hours **Servings:** 4-6 **Difficulty:** Easy

Ingredients:

- 4 cups coconut water
- 1/4 cup water kefir grains
- 1 lime, juiced.
- 1 tablespoon fresh mint leaves, chopped.
- 1 teaspoon maple syrup (optional)

Instructions:

1. Combine the coconut water and water kefir grains in a clean jar. Cover the pot with a breathable cloth and secure it with a rubber band.

2. Let the mixture ferment at room temperature for 24-48 hours. The longer the fermentation time, the stronger and tangier the kefir.

3. After fermentation, strain the kefir grains from the liquid using a fine-mesh strainer. Then, set aside the kefir grains for future batches.

4. Stir in the lime juice, fresh mint leaves, and maple syrup (if using). Taste and adjust the sweetness and acidity as desired.

5. Chill the kefir in the refrigerator for at least an hour before serving.

Nutritional Values: Calories: 45 Fat: 0g Carbohydrates: 11g Fiber: 0g Protein: 0g Sodium: 30mg

151. Probiotic Bowl with Brown Rice, Tempeh, And Fermented Vegetables

Preparation time: 10 minutes **Cooking Time:** 25 minutes **Servings:** 4 **Difficulty:** Easy

Ingredients:

- 2 cups cooked brown rice.
- 1 block tempeh, cut into cubes.
- 1 tablespoon olive oil
- 1 teaspoon smoked paprika.
- 1/2 teaspoon salt
- 1/4 teaspoon black pepper
- 2 cups mixed fermented vegetables (such as sauerkraut, pickles, or kimchi)
- 1 avocado, sliced.
- 1/4 cup pumpkin seeds
- 1/4 cup chopped fresh cilantro.
- 1 lime, cut into wedges.

Instructions:

1. Preheat the oven to 375°F (190°C). Line a baking sheet with parchment paper.

2. Toss the cubed tempeh with olive oil, smoked paprika, salt, and black pepper in a bowl.

3. Spread the tempeh out in a single layer on the prepared baking sheet. Bake for 25 minutes or until golden and crispy.

4. To assemble the bowls, divide the cooked brown rice among four bowls. Top each bowl with the roasted tempeh, mixed fermented vegetables, sliced avocado, and pumpkin seeds.

5. Garnish each bowl with fresh cilantro and a lime wedge.

Nutritional Values: Calories: 374kcal Fat: 21g Carbohydrates: 34g Fiber: 12g Sugar: 2g Protein: 16g

152. Pickled Beets with Fresh Dill and Apple Cider Vinegar

Preparation time: 10 minutes **Cooking Time:** 30-40 minutes **Servings:** 4-6 **Difficulty:** Easy
Ingredients:
- 4 medium-sized beets peeled and sliced.
- 1/2 cup apple cider vinegar
- 1/2 cup water
- 1 tablespoon sugar
- 1/2 teaspoon salt
- 1/4 teaspoon black pepper
- 1 tablespoon fresh dill, chopped.

Instructions:
1. Preheat oven to 400°F (200°C).
2. Peel the beets and slice them into rounds.
3. Place the beet slices on a baking sheet and roast for 30-40 minutes or until tender.
4. While the beets are roasting, prepare the pickling liquid. Combine the apple cider vinegar, water, sugar, salt, and black pepper in a small saucepan.
5. Bring the mixture to a boil over medium-high heat, stirring occasionally to dissolve the sugar and salt.
6. Reduce the heat to low and simmer for 5 minutes.
7. Once the beets are tender, remove them from the oven and let them cool slightly.

8. Transfer the roasted beets to a large glass jar or container.
9. Pour the pickling liquid over the beets, ensuring they are completely covered.
10. Add the fresh dill to the jar or container.
11. Cover the jar or container tightly and refrigerate for at least 2 hours before serving.
12. Serve cold as a side dish or add to salads.

Nutritional Values: Calories: 60 Fat: 0g Carbohydrates: 14g Fiber: 3g Protein: 2g Sodium: 210mg

153. Probiotic Drink with Kefir, Blueberries, And Honey

Preparation time: 5 minutes **Servings:** 1 **Difficulty:** Easy
Ingredients:
- 1 cup low FODMAP kefir
- 1/2 cup blueberries
- 1 tsp honey
- Ice cubes (optional)

Instructions:
1. Add the kefir, blueberries, and honey to a blender and blend until smooth.
2. Taste and adjust sweetness as needed.
3. If desired, add ice cubes to the blender and mix again.
4. Pour into a glass and enjoy immediately.

Nutritional Values: Calories: 167 kcal Fat: 2g Carbohydrates: 31g Fiber: 2g Sugar: 25g Protein: 8g

Smoothies

154. Probiotic Drink with Kefir, Blueberries, And Honey

Preparation time: 5 minutes **Servings:** 1
Difficulty: Easy
Ingredients:

- 1 cup low FODMAP kefir
- 1/2 cup blueberries
- 1 tsp honey
- Ice cubes (optional)

Instructions:

1. Add the kefir, blueberries, and honey to a blender and blend until smooth.
2. Taste and adjust sweetness as needed.
3. If desired, add ice cubes to the blender and mix again.
4. Pour into a glass and enjoy immediately.

Nutritional Values: Calories: 167 kcal Fat: 2g Carbohydrates: 31g Fiber: 2g Sugar: 25g Protein: 8g

155. Blueberry Smoothie with Almond Milk and Spinach

Preparation time: 5 minutes **Servings:** 1
Difficulty: Easy
Ingredients:

- 1 cup fresh spinach leaves
- 1/2 cup fresh blueberries
- 1/2 banana (frozen or fresh)
- 1 cup unsweetened almond milk
- 1 tbsp almond butter
- 1 tbsp chia seeds
- Ice (optional)

Instructions:

1. Rinse the spinach and blueberries and chop the banana into small pieces.
2. Add the spinach, blueberries, banana, almond milk, almond butter, and chia seeds to a blender.
3. Blend until smooth and creamy, adding ice if you want a thicker consistency.
4. Pour the smoothie into a glass and enjoy immediately.

Nutritional Values: Calories: 225 Fat: 12.3 g Carbohydrates: 25.3 g Fiber: 9.6 g Protein: 7.3 g Sodium: 123 mg Potassium: 547 mg Sugar: 10.4 g

156. Green Smoothie with Kiwi, Banana, And Spinach

Preparation time: 5 minutes **Cooking Time:** None **Servings:** 1 **Difficulty:** Easy
Ingredients:

- 1 kiwi peeled and chopped.
- 1/2 ripe banana, sliced.
- 1 cup spinach leaves, packed.
- 1/2 cup unsweetened almond milk
- 1/2 cup ice
- 1 tablespoon chia seeds (optional)

Instructions:

1. Add all ingredients to a blender and blend until smooth.
2. If the smoothie is too thick, add more almond milk or water to thin it out.
3. Pour into a glass and enjoy immediately.

Nutritional Values: Calories: 170 kcal Fat: 5g Carbohydrates: 31g Fiber: 9g Protein: 4g

157. Mixed Berry Smoothie

107

with Almond Milk and Chia Seeds

Preparation time: 5 minutes **Cooking Time:** None **Servings:** 2 **Difficulty:** Easy

Ingredients:

- 1 cup mixed berries (strawberries, blueberries, raspberries, etc.)
- 1 banana
- 1 cup unsweetened almond milk
- 1 tablespoon chia seeds
- 1 tablespoon maple syrup (optional)

Instructions:

1. Wash and chop the mixed berries and bananas.
2. Add the mixed berries, banana, almond milk, chia seeds, and maple syrup (optional) to a blender.
3. Blend until smooth and creamy.
4. Pour into glasses and serve immediately.

Nutritional Values: Calories: 127 kcal Fat: 3.9g Carbohydrates: 23.4g Fiber: 7.1g Protein: 2.9g Sodium: 89mg

158.   Peach And Almond Milk Smoothie with Ginger and Turmeric

Preparation time: 5 minutes **Servings:** 1 **Difficulty:** Easy

Ingredients:

- 1 ripe peach pitted and chopped.
- 1 cup unsweetened almond milk
- 1/2-inch piece of fresh ginger, peeled and chopped.
- 1/4 tsp ground turmeric
- 1 tbsp maple syrup (optional)
- 1/2 cup ice cubes

Instructions:

1. Add the chopped peach, almond milk, ginger, turmeric, and maple syrup (if using) to a blender.
2. Blend on high until smooth.
3. Add the ice cubes and blend again until smooth.
4. Pour the smoothie into a glass and enjoy!

Nutritional Values: Calories: 140kcal Protein: 3g Fat: 4g Saturated Fat: 0.3g Carbohydrates: 28g Fiber: 4g Sugar: 20g Sodium: 180mg

159.   Pineapple And Coconut Milk Smoothie with Spinach

Preparation time: 5 minutes **Cooking Time:** None **Servings:** 1 **Difficulty:** Easy

Ingredients:

- 1 cup fresh spinach
- 1 cup frozen pineapple chunks
- 1/2 cup canned coconut milk (unsweetened)
- 1/2 cup unsweetened almond milk
- 1 tablespoon chia seeds
- 1 tablespoon maple syrup (optional)

Instructions:

1. Add spinach, frozen pineapple, coconut, almond, and chia seeds to a blender.
2. Blend until smooth and creamy.
3. Taste the smoothie and add maple syrup, if desired, for sweetness.
4. Pour the smoothie into a glass and serve immediately.

Nutritional Values: Calories: 290kcal Carbohydrates: 31g Protein: 5g Fat: 20g Saturated Fat: 13g Cholesterol: 0mg Sodium: 145mg Potassium: 593mg Fiber: 7g Sugar: 16g Vitamin A: 3087IU Vitamin C: 70mg Calcium: 320mg Iron: 3mg

160. Mango And Orange Smoothie with Almond Milk

Preparation time: 5 minutes **Cooking Time:** None **Servings:** 2 **Difficulty:** Easy
Ingredients:
- 1 large ripe mango peeled and chopped.
- 1 large orange peeled and segmented.
- 1 cup unsweetened almond milk
- 1 tablespoon chia seeds
- 1 tablespoon maple syrup (optional)
- Ice cubes (optional)

Instructions:
1. Add the chopped mango and orange segments to a blender.
2. Pour in the almond milk and add the chia seeds.
3. If using, add the maple syrup.
4. Blend until smooth and creamy.
5. If desired, add a few ice cubes and blend again until smooth.
6. Pour into glasses and serve chilled.

Nutritional Values: Calories: 139 kcal Fat: 3.3 g Carbohydrates: 27.6 g Fiber: 4.4 g Protein: 2.8 g

161. Blueberry And an Avocado Smoothie with Almond Milk And Spinach

Preparation time: 5 minutes **Servings:** 1 **Difficulty:** Easy
Ingredients:
- 1/2 ripe avocado peeled and pitted.
- 1/2 cup fresh or frozen blueberries
- 1 cup fresh spinach
- 1 cup unsweetened almond milk
- 1 tablespoon maple syrup
- 1/2 teaspoon vanilla extract
- Ice cubes (optional)

Instructions:
1. Add avocado, blueberries, spinach, almond milk, maple syrup, and vanilla extract into a blender.
2. Blend on high until smooth and creamy.
3. Add ice cubes, if desired, and blend again until smooth.
4. Pour into a glass and serve immediately.

Nutritional Values: Calories: 224kcal Total Fat: 14g Saturated Fat: 2g Trans Fat: 0g Cholesterol: 0mg Sodium: 181mg Total Carbohydrates: 24g Dietary Fiber: 7g Sugars: 12g Protein: 4g

162. Chocolate And Almond Milk Smoothie

Preparation time: 5 minutes **Servings:** 1 **Difficulty:** Easy
Ingredients:
- 1 ripe banana
- 1 tablespoon peanut butter
- 1 tablespoon cocoa powder
- 1 cup unsweetened almond milk
- 1/2 teaspoon vanilla extract
- 1-2 ice cubes (optional)

Instructions:
1. Peel the banana and add it to a blender.
2. Add the peanut butter, cocoa powder, almond milk, vanilla extract, and ice cubes (if using) to the blender.
3. Blend the ingredients until smooth.
4. Pour the smoothie into a glass and enjoy!

Nutritional Values: Calories: 220 Fat: 10g Carbohydrates: 30g Fiber: 6g Protein: 6g Sugar: 13g Sodium: 180mg

163. Cherry And Almond

Milk Smoothie with Spinach and Chia Seeds

Preparation time: 5 minutes
Servings: 1
Difficulty: Easy
Ingredients:

- 1 cup frozen cherries
- 1 cup fresh spinach
- 1 tablespoon chia seeds
- 1 tablespoon almond butter
- 1 teaspoon vanilla extract
- 1 cup unsweetened almond milk

Instructions:

1. Add all ingredients to a blender and blend until smooth.
2. Add more almond milk as needed to reach desired consistency.
3. Pour into a glass and enjoy immediately.

Nutritional Values: Calories: 250 Fat: 12g Carbohydrates: 29g Fiber: 9g Protein: 8g

164. Pumpkin And Almond Milk Smoothie with Cinnamon and Nutmeg

Preparation time: 5 minutes **Cooking Time:** 0 minutes **Servings:** 1 **Difficulty:** Easy

Ingredients:

- 1 cup unsweetened almond milk
- 1/2 cup canned pumpkin puree (make sure it's 100% pumpkin with no added sugars)
- 1 banana, sliced.
- 1/2 tsp ground cinnamon
- 1/4 tsp ground nutmeg
- 1 tbsp maple syrup (optional for sweetness)
- Ice cubes (optional)

Instructions:

1. Add the almond milk, pumpkin puree, banana, cinnamon, and nutmeg to a blender.
2. Add the maple syrup and a handful of ice cubes to the blender if desired.
3. Blend until smooth and creamy.
4. Pour into a glass and serve.

Nutritional Values: Calories: 150 kcal Carbohydrates: 30 g Protein: 3 g Fat: 4 g Saturated Fat: 0.2 g Cholesterol: 0 mg Fiber: 6 g Sugar: 16 g Sodium: 157 mg

Seafood

165.   Lemon And Herb Baked Salmon with Green Beans

Preparation time: 10 minutes **Cooking Time:** 20 minutes **Servings:** 4 **Difficulty:** Easy
Ingredients:
- 4 salmon fillets
- 2 tbsp olive oil
- 2 tbsp fresh lemon juice
- 1 tbsp fresh thyme leaves
- 1 tbsp fresh rosemary leaves, chopped.
- Salt and black pepper, to taste
- 400g green beans, trimmed.
- 2 tbsp butter

Instructions:
1. Preheat the oven to 200°C (400°F) and line a baking dish with parchment paper.
2. Rinse the salmon fillets and pat them dry with paper towels. Arrange the fillets in the prepared baking dish.
3. Whisk together the olive oil, lemon juice, thyme, rosemary, salt, and black pepper in a small bowl.
4. Spoon the herb mixture over the salmon fillets, making sure they are well coated.
5. Bake the salmon in the oven for 15-20 minutes or until the flesh is opaque and flakes easily with a fork.
6. While the salmon is cooking, prepare the green beans. Bring a large pot of salted water to a boil. Add the green beans and cook for 4-5 minutes or until tender. Drain the beans and transfer them to a large bowl.
7. Melt the butter in a small saucepan over medium heat.
8. Drizzle the melted butter over the cooked green beans and toss to coat.
9. Serve the baked salmon with the green beans on the side.

Nutritional Values: Calories: 360kcal Fat: 23g Carbohydrates: 9g Protein: 28g Fiber: 4g Sugar: 4g Sodium: 205mg

166.   Garlic And Herb Shrimp with Quinoa

Preparation time: 10 minutes **Cooking Time:** 20 minutes **Servings:** 2 **Difficulty:** Easy
Ingredients:
- 1 cup quinoa
- 2 cups water
- 1 lb. large shrimp peeled and deveined.
- 2 tbsp garlic-infused oil
- 1 tsp dried basil
- 1 tsp dried oregano
- Salt and pepper to taste
- 2 cups green beans, trimmed.
- 1 tbsp olive oil
- 1 tbsp lemon juice
- 1 tbsp chopped fresh parsley.

Instructions:
1. Rinse quinoa thoroughly in a fine-mesh strainer and place it in a saucepan with 2 cups of water. Bring to a boil over high heat, then reduce the heat and let it simmer for about 15 minutes, or until the water is absorbed and the quinoa is tender.
2. Toss the shrimp with garlic-infused oil, dried basil, oregano, salt, and pepper until well-coated.
3. Heat a large skillet over medium-high heat. Add the shrimp to the skillet and

cook on each side for 2-3 minutes until pink and opaque.

4. Steam the green beans in a separate pot until tender while the shrimp is cooking.

5. Whisk together the olive oil, lemon juice, and chopped fresh parsley in a small bowl to make a dressing.

6. Divide the cooked quinoa between two plates. Top with cooked shrimp and steamed green beans. Drizzle with the dressing and serve immediately.

Nutritional Values: Calories: 495kcal Protein: 44g Fat: 17g Carbohydrates: 44g Fiber: 8g

167. Salmon And Mixed Vegetable Stir-Fry with Gluten-Free Soy Sauce

Preparation time: 15 minutes **Cooking Time:** 15 minutes **Servings:** 4 **Difficulty:** Easy
Ingredients:
- 4 salmon fillets
- 2 tablespoons garlic-infused oil
- 1 red bell pepper, sliced.
- 1 zucchini, sliced.
- 1 cup snow peas
- 2 cups bok choy, chopped.
- 1 tablespoon grated ginger
- 1/4 cup gluten-free soy sauce
- 1 tablespoon sesame oil
- Salt and pepper, to taste

Instructions:
1. Preheat a large skillet over medium-high heat.
2. Season the salmon fillets with salt and pepper.
3. Add the garlic-infused oil to the skillet and cook the salmon fillets for 3-4 minutes on each side or until fully

cooked. Remove from the skillet and set aside.

4. Add the red bell pepper, zucchini, snow peas, bok choy, and grated ginger in the same skillet. Stir-fry for 2-3 minutes or until the vegetables are tender.

5. Mix the gluten-free soy sauce and sesame oil in a small bowl.

6. Add the cooked salmon to the skillet with the vegetables and pour the soy sauce mixture over the top.

7. Stir everything together and cook for another 1-2 minutes or until the sauce is heated.

8. Serve immediately with a side of quinoa or brown rice, if desired.

Nutritional Values: Calories: 291 kcal Protein: 28 g Fat: 16 g Carbohydrates: 9 g Fiber: 2 g Sugar: 4 g Sodium: 778 mg

168. Grilled Shrimp Skewers with Zucchini and Cherry Tomatoes

Preparation time: 20 minutes **Cooking Time:** 8-10 minutes **Servings:** 4 **Difficulty:** Easy
Ingredients:
- 1 lb. large shrimp peeled and deveined.
- 2 medium zucchinis, sliced into 1/2-inch rounds.
- 1-pint cherry tomatoes
- 2 tablespoons garlic-infused oil
- 1 tablespoon fresh parsley, chopped.
- Salt and pepper to taste
- Lemon wedges for serving.

Instructions:
1. Preheat the grill to medium-high heat.
2. Whisk together garlic-infused oil, parsley, salt, and pepper in a small bowl.

3. Thread shrimp, zucchini, and cherry tomatoes onto skewers, alternating each ingredient.
4. Brush the skewers with the garlic-infused oil mixture.
5. Grill skewers on each side for 3-4 minutes until the shrimp are pink and cooked through.
6. Remove from the grill and serve with lemon wedges.

Nutritional Values: Calories: 160kcal Fat: 6g Carbohydrates: 7g Protein: 20g Fiber: 2g Sodium: 200mg

169. Pan-Seared Scallops with Roasted Asparagus

Preparation time: 10 minutes **Cooking Time:** 15 minutes **Servings:** 2 **Difficulty:** Easy
Ingredients:
- 1 lb. fresh sea scallops patted dry.
- 1/2 tsp sea salt
- 1/4 tsp black pepper
- 1 tbsp garlic-infused oil
- 1 tbsp butter or ghee
- 1 bunch, asparagus, trimmed.
- 1 tbsp olive oil
- 1/2 tsp dried thyme

Instructions:
1. Preheat the oven to 400°F (200°C).
2. Season the scallops with sea salt and black pepper on both sides.
3. Heat the garlic-infused oil and butter in a large skillet over medium-high heat. When hot, add the scallops in a single layer and cook for 2-3 minutes on each side until golden brown and cooked through. Transfer to a plate and keep warm.
4. Toss the asparagus with olive oil and thyme on a baking sheet. Roast for 10-

12 minutes, until tender and lightly browned.
5. Serve the scallops with the roasted asparagus on the side.

Nutritional Values: Calories: 255 kcal Fat: 15 g Carbohydrates: 8 g Fiber: 3 g Protein: 22 g Sodium: 590 mg

170. Tuna And Cucumber Sushi Roll with Gluten-Free Soy Sauce

Preparation time: 20 minutes **Cooking Time:** 15 minutes (for rice) **Servings:** 4 **Difficulty:** Medium
Ingredients:
- 1 cup sushi rice
- 1 1/2 cups water
- 2 tablespoons rice vinegar
- 2 teaspoons sugar
- 1/2 teaspoon salt
- 4 sheets nori
- 1 can of tuna, drained and flaked.
- 1/2 cucumber, julienned
- Gluten-free soy sauce (for dipping)

Instructions:
1. Rinse the sushi rice in cold water until the water runs clear. Drain well and transfer the rice to a saucepan with 1 1/2 cups of water.
2. Bring the rice to a boil, reduce the heat to low, and cover the saucepan with a tight-fitting lid. Cook for 15 minutes or until the rice is tender and the water has been absorbed.
3. Combine the rice vinegar, sugar, and salt in a small saucepan. Heat gently, stirring constantly, until the sugar has dissolved.

4. Transfer the cooked rice to a large mixing bowl and pour the vinegar mixture over the top. Use a wooden spoon or spatula to gently fold the mixture into the rice until evenly distributed.

5. Lay out a sheet of nori, shiny side down, on a bamboo sushi mat. Then, using a damp spoon or your hands, spread an even layer of rice over the nori, leaving a 1-inch border at the top.

6. Arrange some flaked tuna and julienned cucumber in a line across the center of the rice.

7. Use the bamboo mat to tightly roll up the nori, starting at the bottom and rolling away from you.

8. Repeat with the remaining ingredients to make 4 sushi rolls.

9. Cut each roll into 6-8 pieces using a sharp knife.

10. Serve with gluten-free soy sauce for dipping.

Nutritional Values: Calories: 258 kcal Carbohydrates: 49 g Protein: 9 g Fat: 1 g Fiber: 2 g Sugar: 2 g Sodium: 357 mg

171. Baked Cod with Cherry Tomatoes and Olives

Preparation time: 10 minutes **Cooking Time:** 25-30 minutes **Servings:** 4 **Difficulty:** Easy
Ingredients:
- 4 cod fillets (about 6 ounces each)
- 1-pint cherry tomatoes, halved
- 1/2 cup kalamata olives, pitted and halved.
- 2 tablespoons olive oil
- 1 tablespoon lemon juice
- 1 tablespoon chopped fresh parsley.
- 1 tablespoon chopped fresh oregano.

- Salt and pepper to taste
Instructions:
1. Preheat the oven to 400°F.
2. Toss the cherry tomatoes, olives, olive oil, lemon juice, parsley, oregano, salt, and pepper in a mixing bowl.
3. Place the cod fillets in a baking dish and season with salt and pepper.
4. Spoon the tomato and olive mixture over the cod fillets.
5. Bake in the oven for 25-30 minutes until the fish is cooked and flakes easily with a fork.
6. Remove from the oven and serve immediately.

Nutritional Values: Calories: 243 kcal Fat: 11g Carbohydrates: 6g Protein: 29g Fiber: 2g Sodium: 386mg

172. Shrimp And Mixed Vegetable Kebabs with Gluten-Free Marinade

Preparation time: 20 minutes **Cooking Time:** 10 minutes **Servings:** 4 **Difficulty:** Easy
Ingredients:
- 1-pound large shrimp, peeled and deveined
- 2 bell peppers, cut into 1-inch pieces.
- 1 zucchini, sliced.
- 1 yellow squash, sliced.
- 1/4 cup olive oil
- 2 tablespoons gluten-free soy sauce
- 1 tablespoon maple syrup
- 1 tablespoon Dijon mustard
- 1 tablespoon lemon juice
- 1 teaspoon smoked paprika.
- Salt and pepper, to taste
- Wooden skewers
Instructions:

1. Soak the wooden skewers in water for at least 30 minutes to prevent burning.
2. Mix the olive oil, soy sauce, maple syrup, Dijon mustard, lemon juice, smoked paprika, salt, and pepper to make the marinade.
3. Thread the shrimp, bell peppers, zucchini, and yellow squash onto the skewers, alternating the ingredients.
4. Brush the kebabs with the marinade and let them marinate for 10-15 minutes.
5. Preheat the grill to medium-high heat.
6. Grill the kebabs for 3-4 minutes per side until the shrimp are pink and cooked through and the vegetables are slightly charred.
7. Serve the kebabs hot, with additional marinade on the side if desired.

Nutritional Values: Calories: 270 kcal Fat: 15g Carbohydrates: 12g Fiber: 3g Protein: 22g Crab and avocado salad with mixed greens and gluten-free dressing

Preparation time: 20 minutes **Cooking Time:** N/A **Servings:** 2-3 **Difficulty:** Easy

Ingredients:

- 6 oz canned crab meat, drained and rinsed.
- 1 large avocado, diced.
- 4 cups mixed greens
- 1/2 cup cherry tomatoes, halved.
- 1/4 cup sliced almonds.
- 2 tbsp chopped fresh cilantro.
- 2 tbsp olive oil
- 1 tbsp lemon juice
- 1 tbsp gluten-free Dijon mustard
- Salt and pepper to taste

Instructions:

1. Combine the crab meat, avocado, mixed greens, cherry tomatoes, sliced almonds, and cilantro in a large mixing bowl.
2. Whisk the olive oil, lemon juice, Dijon mustard, and salt and pepper in a small mixing bowl to taste.
3. Pour the dressing over the salad and toss well to coat.
4. Divide the salad between 2-3 plates and serve immediately.

Nutritional Values: Calories: 318 Fat: 27g Carbohydrates: 13g Fiber: 7g Protein: 12g

173.   Seared Tuna Steak with Green Beans and Gluten-Free Soy Sauce

Preparation time: 10 minutes **Cooking Time:** 15 minutes **Servings:** 2 **Difficulty:** Easy

Ingredients:

- 2 tuna steaks (about 6 oz each)
- Salt and pepper, to taste
- 1 tablespoon garlic-infused oil
- 8 oz green beans, trimmed.
- 1 tablespoon gluten-free soy sauce
- 1 tablespoon lemon juice
- 1 teaspoon honey
- 1 teaspoon sesame seeds

Instructions:

1. Season the tuna steaks with salt and pepper on both sides.
2. Heat the garlic-infused oil in a large non-stick pan over medium-high heat.
3. Once the pan is hot, add the tuna steaks and sear for 2-3 minutes on each side or until browned and cooked to your liking.
4. Remove the tuna from the pan and set it aside.
5. Add the trimmed green beans to the same pan and sauté for 5-7 minutes or until tender-crisp.

6. Whisk together the gluten-free soy sauce, lemon juice, honey, and sesame seeds in a small bowl to make the dressing.
7. To serve, divide the green beans between two plates, top each dish with a tuna steak, and drizzle the dressing.

Nutritional Values: Calories: 250 kcal Fat: 9 g Carbohydrates: 10 g Fiber: 3 g Protein: 32 g Roasted salmon with mixed vegetables and gluten-free teriyaki sauce

174. Roasted Salmon with Mixed Vegetables and Teriyaki Sauce

Preparation time: 15 minutes **Cooking Time:** 20 minutes **Servings:** 4 **Difficulty:** Easy
Ingredients:
- 4 salmon fillets
- 1 large zucchini, sliced.
- 1 red bell pepper, sliced.
- 1 yellow bell pepper, sliced.
- 1 tablespoon garlic-infused olive oil
- Salt and black pepper, to taste
- 1 tablespoon sesame seeds
- 1 tablespoon chopped scallions.

For the teriyaki sauce:
- 1/4 cup gluten-free soy sauce
- 1/4 cup rice vinegar
- 2 tablespoons maple syrup
- 1 tablespoon grated ginger
- 1 tablespoon cornstarch
- 1/4 cup water

Instructions:
1. Preheat the oven to 400°F (200°C). Line a baking sheet with parchment paper.
2. Whisk together all the ingredients for the teriyaki sauce in a small bowl.
3. Toss the sliced zucchini, red bell pepper, and yellow bell pepper with garlic-infused olive oil, salt, and black pepper in a large bowl.
4. Spread the vegetables on the prepared baking sheet, leaving enough room for the salmon fillets.
5. Place the salmon fillets on the baking sheet with the vegetables. Brush each fillet with teriyaki sauce, reserving some sauce for later.
6. Bake for 15-20 minutes or until the salmon is cooked through and the vegetables are tender.
7. In a small saucepan, heat the remaining teriyaki sauce until thickened.
8. Sprinkle the roasted vegetables and salmon with sesame seeds and chopped scallions. Serve with the teriyaki sauce on the side.

Nutritional Values: Calories: 350 kcal Fat: 18g Carbohydrates: 12g Fiber: 2g Protein: 33g Sodium: 618mg

175. Shrimp And Mixed Vegetable Stir-Fry with Gluten-Free Oyster Sauce

Preparation time: 15 minutes **Cooking Time:** 15 minutes **Servings:** 4 **Difficulty:** Easy
Ingredients:
- 1 lb. raw shrimp peeled and deveined.
- 2 cups mixed vegetables (bell peppers, carrots, bok choy, and zucchini), sliced.
- 2 tbsp garlic-infused oil
- 2 tbsp gluten-free oyster sauce
- 1 tbsp gluten-free soy sauce
- 1 tbsp rice vinegar
- 1 tsp cornstarch
- Salt and pepper, to taste

- 2 cups cooked quinoa for serving.

Instructions:

1. Whisk together the gluten-free oyster sauce, gluten-free soy sauce, rice vinegar, and cornstarch in a small bowl. Set aside.
2. Heat the garlic-infused oil in a large skillet or wok over medium-high heat.
3. Add the mixed vegetables and stir-fry for 5-7 minutes, until tender.
4. Add the shrimp to the skillet and cook for 2-3 minutes, until pink and cooked.
5. Pour the sauce over the shrimp and vegetables and stir to coat.
6. Cook for an additional 1-2 minutes, until the sauce has thickened, and everything is well coated.
7. Season with salt and pepper to taste.
8. Serve the shrimp and vegetable stir-fry over cooked quinoa.

Nutritional Values: Calories: 258 kcal Fat: 7.2 g Carbohydrates: 27.3 g Fiber: 4.3 g Protein: 22.5 g

176. Baked Tilapia with Lemon and Dill Seasoning

Preparation time: 10 minutes **Cooking Time:** 20 minutes **Servings:** 4 **Difficulty:** Easy
Ingredients:

- 4 tilapia fillets
- 2 tablespoons olive oil
- 2 tablespoons fresh lemon juice
- 1 teaspoon dried dill
- Salt and pepper to taste
- Lemon wedges for serving.

Instructions:

1. Preheat the oven to 375°F (190°C).
2. Pat the tilapia fillets dry with a paper towel and place them on a baking sheet.

3. Whisk together the olive oil, lemon juice, dried dill, salt, and pepper in a small bowl.
4. Brush the mixture over the tilapia fillets, ensuring they are evenly coated.
5. Bake the tilapia for 15-20 minutes until it is cooked and flakes quickly with a fork.
6. Serve the tilapia hot with lemon wedges.

Nutritional Values: Calories: 154 kcal Fat: 7g Carbohydrates: 0g Protein: 22g Fiber: 0g Sodium: 54mg

177. Grilled Salmon with Roasted Sweet Potatoes and Broccoli

Preparation time: 15 minutes **Cooking Time:** 25 minutes **Servings:** 4 **Difficulty:** Easy
Ingredients:

- 4 salmon fillets (about 6 oz each)
- 2 medium-sized sweet potatoes peeled and diced.
- 2 cups broccoli florets
- 2 tbsp olive oil
- Salt and pepper to taste
- 1 tsp garlic-infused olive oil
- 2 tbsp fresh parsley, chopped.
- Lemon wedges for serving.

Instructions:

1. Preheat the oven to 400°F. Line a baking sheet with parchment paper.
2. Toss the diced sweet potatoes and broccoli florets with olive oil, salt, and pepper. Spread the vegetables on the prepared baking sheet and roast for 20-25 minutes or until tender.
3. Heat a grill pan over medium-high heat. Brush the salmon fillets with garlic-

infused olive oil and season with salt and pepper.

4. Place the salmon fillets on the grill pan, skin side down. Grill for 3-4 minutes or until the skin is crispy. Flip the salmon and grill for 2-3 minutes or until cooked.

5. Divide the roasted sweet potatoes and broccoli between 4 plates. Top with a grilled salmon fillet.

6. Garnish with chopped parsley and serve with lemon wedges.

Nutritional Values: Calories: 353kcal Fat: 16g Carbohydrates: 16g Fiber: 3g Protein: 36g Sugar: 4g Sodium: 159mg

178. Shrimp And Mixed Vegetable Curry with Gluten-Free Coconut Milk

Preparation time: 15 minutes **Cooking Time:** 25 minutes **Servings:** 4 **Difficulty:** Easy

Ingredients:
- 1 pound shrimp peeled and deveined.
- 1 red bell pepper, sliced.
- 1 zucchini, sliced.
- 1 yellow squash, sliced.
- 1 cup green beans, trimmed.
- 1 tablespoon garlic-infused olive oil
- 1 tablespoon curry powder
- 1/2 teaspoon ground ginger
- 1/4 teaspoon ground turmeric
- 1 can (13.5 ounces) full-fat coconut milk
- Salt and pepper, to taste
- Fresh cilantro leaves, chopped (optional)

Instructions:
1. Heat the garlic-infused olive oil in a large skillet over medium heat.

2. Add the red bell pepper, zucchini, yellow squash, and green beans to the skillet. Cook for 5-7 minutes or until the vegetables are tender.

3. Add the curry powder, ginger, and turmeric to the skillet. Stir to combine and cook for 1-2 minutes.

4. Pour the coconut milk into the skillet and stir until everything is combined.

5. Bring the mixture to a simmer and cook for 10-12 minutes or until the sauce has thickened slightly.

6. Add the shrimp to the skillet and cook for 5-7 minutes or until the shrimp are pink and cooked through.

7. Season with salt and pepper to taste.

8. Serve the curry hot, garnished with fresh cilantro leaves, if desired.

Nutritional Values: Calories: 315kcal Carbohydrates: 12g Protein: 26g Fat: 19g Fiber: 4g Sugar: 4g Sodium: 156mg

179. Crab And Corn Chowder with Broth

Preparation time: 15 minutes **Cooking Time:** 35 minutes **Servings:** 4 **Difficulty:** Easy

Ingredients:
- 2 tablespoons garlic-infused oil
- 2 tablespoons gluten-free flour
- 1 cup low FODMAP chicken broth
- 2 cups lactose-free milk
- 1 teaspoon paprika
- 1 teaspoon dried thyme
- 1 bay leaf
- 2 cups fresh or frozen corn kernels
- 1-pound cooked crabmeat
- 2 tablespoons chopped fresh parsley.
- Salt and pepper to taste

Instructions:

1. Heat the garlic-infused oil in a large pot over medium heat.
2. Add the gluten-free flour and whisk for 1-2 minutes until the mixture turns golden brown.
3. Slowly whisk in the low-FODMAP chicken broth and lactose-free milk.
4. Add the paprika, dried thyme, and bay leaf.
5. Add the corn kernels and bring the mixture to a simmer.
6. Let the mixture simmer for 20-25 minutes or until the corn is tender.
7. Add the cooked crabmeat and simmer for another 5 minutes.
8. Remove the bay leaf and season with salt and pepper to taste.
9. Serve the chowder hot, garnished with chopped fresh parsley.

Nutritional Values: Calories: 360 kcal Fat: 9 g Carbohydrates: 36 g Fiber: 3 g Protein: 34 g

180. Pan-Seared Halibut with Mixed Vegetables and Sauce

Preparation time: 10 minutes **Cooking Time:** 20 minutes **Servings:** 4 **Difficulty:** Easy

Ingredients:
- 4 halibut fillets (4-6 ounces each)
- 2 tablespoons olive oil
- Salt and pepper to taste
- 1 red bell pepper, sliced.
- 1 yellow squash, sliced.
- 1 zucchini, sliced.
- 1/2 cup cherry tomatoes, halved.
- 2 tablespoons chopped fresh parsley.
- 2 tablespoons chopped fresh basil.
- 1 tablespoon gluten-free soy sauce
- 1 tablespoon lemon juice
- 1 tablespoon honey
- 1 teaspoon Dijon mustard

Instructions:
1. Season halibut fillets with salt and pepper on both sides.
2. Heat olive oil in a large skillet over medium-high heat. Add the halibut fillets and cook for 4-5 minutes on each side or until the fish is cooked through and opaque.
3. While the halibut is cooking, prepare the vegetables. In a separate skillet, sauté the sliced bell pepper, squash, and zucchini until tender.
4. Add the halved cherry tomatoes to the vegetable skillet and sauté for 1-2 minutes.
5. In a small bowl, whisk together the soy sauce, lemon juice, honey, and Dijon mustard to make the gluten-free sauce.
6. Once the halibut is cooked, remove it from the skillet and set it aside on a plate.
7. Add the cooked vegetables to the skillet with the gluten-free sauce and stir to coat.
8. Place the halibut fillets back in the skillet with the vegetables and sauce, and heat for 1-2 minutes.
9. Serve hot, garnished with chopped parsley and basil.

Nutritional Values: Calories: 255kcal Fat: 11g Carbohydrates: 11g Fiber: 2g Sugar: 7g Protein: 27g

181. Salmon And Mixed Vegetable Foil Packets with Lemon and Herbs

Preparation time: 15 minutes **Cooking Time:** 20 minutes **Servings:** 4 **Difficulty:** Easy

Ingredients:

- 4 skinless salmon fillets
- 2 zucchinis, sliced.
- 1 red bell pepper, sliced.
- 1 yellow bell pepper, sliced.
- 1/2 cup cherry tomatoes
- 2 tablespoons olive oil
- 2 tablespoons fresh lemon juice
- 2 tablespoons chopped fresh herbs (such as parsley, thyme, or dill)
- Salt and pepper, to taste

Instructions:

1. Preheat the oven to 400°F (200°C).
2. Cut 4 pieces of aluminum foil (about 12 inches long) and place them on a baking sheet.
3. Divide the sliced zucchini, bell peppers, and cherry tomatoes evenly among the foil packets.
4. Season the vegetables with salt and pepper, then drizzle them with 1 tablespoon olive oil.
5. Season the salmon fillets with salt and pepper, then place one fillet on the vegetables in each packet.
6. Whisk together the remaining olive oil, lemon juice, and chopped herbs in a small bowl. Drizzle the mixture over the salmon fillets.
7. Fold the foil up around the salmon and vegetables to create sealed packets.
8. Bake the packets in the oven for 20 minutes or until the salmon is cooked and the vegetables are tender.
9. Serve hot and enjoy!

Nutritional Values: Calories: 326 kcal Protein: 34 g Fat: 18 g Carbohydrates: 8 g Fiber: 3 g Sugar: 5 g Sodium: 116 mg

182. Shrimp And Zucchini Noodles with Marinara Sauce

Preparation time: 20 minutes **Cooking Time:** 20 minutes **Servings:** 4 **Difficulty:** Easy

Ingredients:

- 4 medium-sized zucchinis, spiralized
- 1 lb. of shrimp peeled and deveined.
- 2 tbsp olive oil
- 1 cup of gluten-free marinara sauce
- 1 tsp dried basil
- 1/2 tsp garlic-infused oil
- Salt and pepper to taste
- Parmesan cheese (optional)

Instructions:

1. In a large pan, heat olive oil over medium-high heat.
2. Add the shrimp to the pan and cook for 2-3 minutes on each side until they turn pink.
3. Remove the shrimp from the pan and set aside.
4. Add the spiralized zucchini noodles to the same pan and cook for 2-3 minutes until they are slightly tender but firm.
5. Add the gluten-free marinara sauce to the pan along with the dried basil, garlic-infused oil, salt, and pepper. Stir to combine.
6. Bring the sauce to a simmer and cook for 5-7 minutes, stirring occasionally.
7. Add the cooked shrimp back to the pan and stir to combine.
8. Serve the shrimp and zucchini noodles with gluten-free marinara sauce and sprinkle with Parmesan cheese if desired.

Nutritional Values: Calories: 180kcal Fat: 9g Saturated fat: 1.4g Cholesterol: 130mg Sodium:

460mg Potassium: 780mg Carbohydrates: 9g
Fiber: 2.5g Sugar: 5g Protein: 17g

183. Baked Sea Bass with Cherry Tomatoes and Capers

Preparation time: 10 minutes **Cooking Time:** 20 minutes **Servings:** 4 **Difficulty:** Easy
Ingredients:

- 4 sea bass fillets (about 6 ounces each)
- 1-pint cherry tomatoes
- 2 tablespoons capers
- 1/4 cup olive oil
- 1/4 cup white wine
- Salt and pepper to taste
- Fresh parsley for garnish

Instructions:

1. Preheat the oven to 375°F.
2. Rinse and pat dry the sea bass fillets.
3. Combine the cherry tomatoes and capers in a large baking dish. Drizzle with olive oil and season with salt and pepper.
4. Place the sea bass fillets on the cherry tomato and caper mixture.
5. Pour the white wine over the sea bass fillets.
6. Bake in the preheated oven for 20 minutes or until the fish is cooked through and flaky.
7. Serve hot with fresh parsley for garnish.

Nutritional Values: Calories: 280 kcal Fat: 15g Carbohydrates: 3g Protein: 32g Sodium: 400mg

Desserts

184.   Chocolate And Peanut Butter Energy Balls

Preparation time: 10 minutes **Cooking Time:** No cooking required **Servings:** 10-12 energy balls **Difficulty:** Easy
Ingredients:

- 1 cup rolled oats.
- 1/2 cup smooth peanut butter (no added sugars)
- 1/4 cup pure maple syrup
- 1/4 cup dark chocolate chips (make sure they are low FODMAP)
- 1/4 cup chia seeds
- 1/4 cup unsweetened shredded coconut
- 1 tsp vanilla extract
- 1/2 tsp cinnamon
- Pinch of salt

Instructions:

1. Add rolled oats, chia seeds, unsweetened shredded coconut, dark chocolate chips, cinnamon, and salt in a mixing bowl. Mix well.
2. Add peanut butter, pure maple syrup, and vanilla extract. Mix until all ingredients are well combined.
3. Using a cookie scoop or spoon, roll the mixture into balls.
4. Place energy balls in an airtight container and refrigerate for at least 30 minutes before serving.
5. Enjoy as a snack or as a pre/post-workout energy booster.

Nutritional Values: Calories: 165 kcal Fat: 9g Carbohydrates: 17g Fiber: 4g Protein: 5g

185.   Banana And Almond Butter Ice Cream

Preparation time: 10 minutes Freezing time: 6 hours **Servings:** 4 **Difficulty:** Easy
Ingredients:

- 2 ripe bananas
- 1/2 cup smooth almond butter
- 1 cup lactose-free milk or almond milk
- 1/4 cup maple syrup
- 1 tsp vanilla extract

Instructions:

1. Peel the bananas and cut them into small pieces.
2. Place the bananas, almond butter, lactose-free milk or almond milk, maple syrup, and vanilla extract in a blender or food processor.
3. Blend until the mixture is smooth and creamy.
4. Pour the mixture into a freezer-safe container and freeze for 2 hours.
5. After 2 hours, remove the container from the freezer and stir the mixture to break up any ice crystals.
6. Return the container to the freezer and freeze for 4 hours or until the ice cream is firm.
7. When ready to serve, let the ice cream sit at room temperature for a few minutes to soften before scooping.

Nutritional Values: Calories: 282 kcal Fat: 18g Carbohydrates: 25g Fiber: 4g Protein: 8g Sodium: 41mg

186.   Blueberry And Oatmeal Breakfast Bars

Preparation time: 10 minutes **Cooking Time:** 30 minutes **Servings:** 8 bars **Difficulty:** Easy
Ingredients:

- 1 cup gluten-free rolled oats.
- 1/2 cup almond flour
- 1/4 cup maple syrup
- 1/4 cup coconut oil, melted.
- 1 egg
- 1 tsp vanilla extract
- 1/2 tsp baking powder
- 1/4 tsp salt
- 1 cup fresh blueberries
- 2 tbsp chia seeds

Instructions:

1. Preheat the oven to 350°F (175°C) and line an 8x8 inch baking dish with parchment paper.
2. Combine the rolled oats, almond flour, baking powder, and salt in a mixing bowl.
3. Mix the maple syrup, melted coconut oil, egg, and vanilla extract until well combined.
4. Add the wet ingredients to the dry ingredients and mix until a dough forms.
5. Fold in the blueberries and chia seeds.
6. Transfer the dough to the prepared baking dish and press down firmly to form an even layer.
7. Bake for 25-30 minutes or until golden brown and set.
8. Let cool in the dish for 10 minutes before slicing into 8 bars.

Nutritional Values: Calories: 218kcal Carbohydrates: 22g Protein: 4g Fat: 14g Saturated Fat: 7g Cholesterol: 23mg Sodium: 107mg Potassium: 146mg Fiber: 4g Sugar: 9g Vitamin A: 57IU Vitamin C: 3mg Calcium: 71mg Iron: 1mg

187.   Pumpkin Pie with Crust

Preparation time: 20 minutes **Cooking Time:** 50 minutes **Servings:** 8 **Difficulty:** Easy
Ingredients:

For the crust:

- 1 1/2 cups gluten-free all-purpose flour
- 1/4 cup coconut oil, melted.
- 1/4 cup maple syrup
- 1/4 tsp salt
- 1/4 tsp cinnamon
- 1/4 tsp nutmeg
- 1/4 tsp ginger
- 1-2 tbsp cold water

For the filling:

- 1 1/2 cups canned pumpkin puree.
- 3/4 cup lactose-free milk
- 1/4 cup maple syrup
- 1 tbsp cornstarch
- 1 tsp cinnamon
- 1/2 tsp ginger
- 1/4 tsp nutmeg
- 1/4 tsp salt
- 2 large eggs, beaten.

Instructions:

1. Preheat oven to 350°F (180°C).
2. Combine the gluten-free flour, melted coconut oil, maple syrup, salt, cinnamon, nutmeg, and ginger in a mixing bowl. Mix until the dough forms into small clumps.
3. Add cold water, one tablespoon until the dough comes together into a ball.
4. Roll out the dough on a sheet of parchment paper until it's about 1/8-inch thick.

5. Transfer the dough to a 9-inch pie dish, pressing it into the bottom and sides of the word. Use a fork to prick the bottom of the crust several times.

6. Bake the crust in the oven for 10-12 minutes or until lightly golden brown.

7. While the crust is baking, make the filling. In a mixing bowl, whisk together the pumpkin puree, lactose-free milk, maple syrup, cornstarch, cinnamon, ginger, nutmeg, salt, and beaten eggs until smooth.

8. Once the crust is done, pour the filling into it and spread it evenly.

9. Bake the pie in the oven for 40-45 minutes or until the filling is set and no longer jiggles in the center.

10. Remove the pie from the oven and let it cool completely before slicing and serving.

Nutritional Values: Calories: 240kcal Fat: 11g Carbohydrates: 30g Fiber: 3g Protein: 5g

188. Chocolate And Almond Flour Brownies

Preparation time: 10 minutes **Cooking Time:** 25 minutes **Servings:** 12 brownies **Difficulty:** Easy

Ingredients:
- 1/2 cup almond flour
- 1/2 cup gluten-free all-purpose flour
- 1/2 cup unsweetened cocoa powder
- 1/2 tsp baking powder
- 1/2 tsp salt
- 1/2 cup coconut oil, melted.
- 1/2 cup maple syrup
- 2 large eggs
- 1 tsp vanilla extract
- 1/4 cup dark chocolate chips

Instructions:

1. Preheat the oven to 350°F and line an 8x8 inch baking pan with parchment paper.

2. Whisk together the almond flour, gluten-free all-purpose flour, cocoa powder, baking powder, and salt in a medium bowl.

3. Whisk together the melted coconut oil and maple syrup in a separate large bowl until well combined.

4. Add the eggs and vanilla extract to the large bowl with the coconut oil mixture and whisk until fully incorporated.

5. Gradually add the dry ingredients to the wet ingredients and stir until combined.

6. Fold in the dark chocolate chips.

7. Pour the batter into the prepared baking pan and smooth the surface with a spatula.

8. Bake for 25 minutes or until a toothpick inserted into the center comes clean.

9. Let the brownies cool completely in the pan, then slice into 12 squares and serve.

Nutritional Values: Calories: 195 Fat: 14g Carbohydrates: 17g Fiber: 3g Sugar: 9g Protein: 4g

189. Lemon And Coconut Flour Cake

Preparation time: 15 minutes **Cooking Time:** 35 minutes **Servings:** 8-10 slices **Difficulty:** Easy

Ingredients:
- 1/2 cup coconut flour
- 1/2 tsp baking powder
- 1/4 tsp salt
- 1/3 cup maple syrup
- 1/3 cup coconut oil, melted.
- 4 eggs

124

- 1/4 cup fresh lemon juice
- Zest of 1 lemon
- 1/4 cup unsweetened almond milk

Instructions:

1. Preheat the oven to 350°F (175°C) and grease an 8-inch round cake pan with coconut oil.
2. Whisk together the coconut flour, baking powder, and salt in a bowl.
3. Mix the maple syrup, melted coconut oil, eggs, lemon juice, lemon zest, and almond milk in another bowl.
4. Add the dry ingredients to the wet ingredients and stir until well combined.
5. Pour the batter into the greased cake pan and smooth the top.
6. Bake for 35 minutes or until a toothpick inserted into the center comes clean.
7. Let the cake cool in the pan for 10 minutes, then remove it and cool completely on a wire rack.
8. Once cooled, slice and serve.

Nutritional Values: Calories: 178 kcal Fat: 13 g Carbohydrates: 12 g Fiber: 4 g Protein: 4 g

190.   Raspberry And Almond Flour Muffins

Preparation time: 15 minutes **Cooking Time:** 25 minutes **Servings:** 12 muffins **Difficulty:** Easy

Ingredients:

- 2 cups almond flour
- 1 tsp baking powder
- 1/2 tsp baking soda
- 1/4 tsp salt
- 1/4 cup maple syrup
- 2 eggs
- 1/4 cup melted coconut oil.
- 1/2 cup almond milk
- 1 tsp vanilla extract

- 1 cup fresh raspberries

Instructions:

1. Preheat the oven to 350°F (180°C) and line a muffin tin with paper liners.
2. Whisk together the almond flour, baking powder, baking soda, and salt in a large bowl.
3. Whisk together the maple syrup, eggs, melted coconut oil, almond milk, and vanilla extract in a separate bowl.
4. Pour the wet ingredients into the dry ingredients and mix until just combined.
5. Gently fold in the fresh raspberries.
6. Spoon the batter into the prepared muffin tin, filling each cup about 3/4 full.
7. Bake for 20-25 minutes or until a toothpick inserted in the center of a muffin comes out clean.
8. Allow the muffins to cool in the tin for 5 minutes, then transfer them to a wire rack to cool completely.

Nutritional Values: Calories: 174 kcal Fat: 14 g Carbohydrates: 8 g Fiber: 2 g Protein: 5 g

191.   Strawberry And Banana Smoothie Bowl with Granola

Preparation time: 10 minutes **Servings:** 2 **Difficulty:** Easy

Ingredients:

For the smoothie:

- 1 cup frozen strawberries
- 1 medium ripe banana
- 1/2 cup almond milk
- 1 tablespoon maple syrup
- 1 teaspoon vanilla extract
- 1/2 teaspoon ground cinnamon
- 1/2 teaspoon ground ginger

For the topping:

- 1/2 cup gluten-free granola

- 1/4 cup sliced strawberries.
- 1/4 cup sliced bananas.

Instructions:

1. Combine the frozen strawberries, banana, almond milk, maple syrup, vanilla extract, cinnamon, and ginger in a blender. Blend until smooth and creamy.
2. Divide the smoothie mixture between two bowls.
3. Top each bowl with gluten-free granola, sliced strawberries, and sliced bananas.
4. Serve immediately and enjoy!

Nutritional Values: Calories: 225 kcal Fat: 5.6 g Carbohydrates: 44 g Fiber: 6 g Protein: 3.7 g

192. Chocolate And Banana Bread with Flour

Preparation time: 15 minutes **Cooking Time:** 50 minutes **Servings:** 12 **Difficulty:** Easy
Ingredients:

- 1 1/2 cups gluten-free all-purpose flour
- 1/2 cup unsweetened cocoa powder
- 1 teaspoon baking powder
- 1/2 teaspoon baking soda
- 1/4 teaspoon salt
- 3 ripe bananas, mashed.
- 2 large eggs
- 1/4 cup maple syrup
- 1/4 cup coconut oil, melted.
- 1/4 cup unsweetened almond milk
- 1 teaspoon vanilla extract
- 1/2 cup dairy-free dark chocolate chips

Instructions:

1. Preheat the oven to 350°F (175°C) and line a 9x5 inch loaf pan with parchment paper.
2. Whisk together the gluten-free flour, cocoa powder, baking powder, baking soda, and salt in a large mixing bowl.

3. Mix the mashed bananas, eggs, maple syrup, melted coconut oil, almond milk, and vanilla extract in a separate bowl.
4. Add the wet ingredients to the dry ingredients and mix until just combined.
5. Fold in the dark chocolate chips.
6. Pour the batter into the prepared loaf pan and smooth the top with a spatula.
7. Bake for 45-50 minutes or until a toothpick inserted in the center comes clean.
8. Let the bread cool in the pan for 10 minutes before transferring it to a wire rack to cool completely.

Nutritional Values: Calories: 200 kcal Fat: 10 g Carbohydrates: 26 g Fiber: 3 g Protein: 4 g

193. Apple And Cinnamon Oatmeal with Almond Milk

Preparation time: 5 minutes **Cooking Time:** 10 minutes **Servings:** 2 **Difficulty:** Easy
Ingredients:

- 1 cup rolled oats.
- 2 cups almond milk
- 1/2 teaspoon cinnamon
- 1/4 teaspoon ginger
- 1/4 teaspoon nutmeg
- 1 tablespoon maple syrup
- 1 medium apple, chopped.
- 1/4 cup chopped pecans (optional)

Instructions:

1. Combine the oats, almond milk, cinnamon, ginger, and nutmeg in a medium saucepan. Stir well.
2. Bring the mixture to a boil over medium-high heat.
3. Reduce the heat to low and simmer, stirring frequently, for 8-10 minutes or until the oatmeal is thick and creamy.

4. Stir in the maple syrup and chopped apple.

5. Divide the oatmeal into two bowls and sprinkle with chopped pecans.

Nutritional Values: Calories: 294 kcal Fat: 10 g Carbohydrates: 44 g Fiber: 8 g Protein: 8 g

194. Mixed Berry and Chia Seed Pudding

Preparation time: 5 minutes cooking time (if any): None **Servings:** 2 **Difficulty:** Easy

Ingredients:

- 1 cup unsweetened almond milk
- 1/4 cup chia seeds
- 1/2 teaspoon vanilla extract
- 1 tablespoon maple syrup
- 1/2 cup mixed berries (e.g., strawberries, blueberries, raspberries)
- 1 tablespoon unsweetened shredded coconut (optional)

Instructions:

1. Whisk together the almond milk, chia seeds, vanilla extract, and maple syrup in a medium bowl until well combined.

2. Let the mixture sit for about 5 minutes, then whisk again to break up clumps.

3. Cover the bowl with plastic wrap or a lid and refrigerate for at least 2 hours or overnight until the pudding thickens.

4. To serve, divide the pudding between 2 bowls or glasses and top with mixed berries and shredded coconut if desired.

Nutritional Values: Calories: 160 Fat: 8g Carbohydrates: 17g Fiber: 10g Protein: 5g Sodium: 65mg

195. Coconut And Almond Flour Cookies

Preparation time: 15 minutes **Cooking Time:** 15-20 minutes **Servings:** 12-15 cookies **Difficulty:** Easy

Ingredients:

- 1 cup almond flour
- 1/4 cup coconut flour
- 1/4 cup coconut oil, melted.
- 1/4 cup pure maple syrup
- 1 egg
- 1/2 tsp vanilla extract
- 1/2 tsp baking powder
- 1/4 tsp salt
- Unsweetened shredded coconut for topping

Instructions:

1. Preheat the oven to 350°F (180°C) and line a baking sheet with parchment paper.

2. Whisk together the almond flour, coconut flour, baking powder, and salt in a medium bowl.

3. Whisk together the melted coconut oil, maple syrup, egg, and vanilla extract in a separate bowl.

4. Add the wet ingredients to the dry ingredients and stir until well combined.

5. Drop the batter onto the prepared baking sheet using a cookie scoop or spoon, leaving about 2 inches between each cookie.

6. Sprinkle shredded coconut on top of each cookie.

7. Bake for 15-20 minutes or until the edges are lightly golden.

8. Allow the cookies to cool on the baking sheet for a few minutes, then transfer them to a wire rack to cool completely.

Nutritional Values: Calories: 110 Total fat: 9g Total carbohydrate: 7g Dietary fiber: 2g Sugars: 4g Protein: 3g

196. Vanilla And Coconut Flour Cupcakes

Preparation time: 15 minutes **Cooking Time:** 20-25 minutes **Servings:** 12 cupcakes **Difficulty:** Easy
Ingredients:

- 1 cup coconut flour
- 1/2 cup gluten-free all-purpose flour
- 1/4 cup tapioca starch
- 1 tsp baking powder
- 1/2 tsp baking soda
- 1/4 tsp salt
- 3/4 cup sugar
- 1/2 cup unsalted butter, softened.
- 2 large eggs
- 1 tsp vanilla extract
- 1 cup lactose-free milk
- 1/2 cup unsweetened shredded coconut

Instructions:

1. Preheat the oven to 350°F (175°C) and line a muffin tin with paper liners.
2. Whisk together the coconut flour, gluten-free flour, tapioca starch, baking powder, baking soda, and salt in a medium bowl.
3. In a separate large bowl, beat the sugar and butter with an electric mixer until light and fluffy. Add the eggs one at a time, beating well after each addition.
4. Mix the vanilla extract with the wet ingredients until combined.
5. Gradually add the dry ingredients to the wet ingredients, alternating with the lactose-free milk, and mix until combined.
6. Fold in the shredded coconut.
7. Scoop the batter into the lined muffin tin, filling each cup 2/3 full.
8. Bake in the preheated oven for 20-25 minutes or until a toothpick inserted into the center of a cupcake comes out clean.
9. Let the cupcakes cool in the muffin tin for 5 minutes, then transfer them to a wire rack to cool completely.

Nutritional Values: Calories: 218kcal Fat: 11g Carbohydrates: 28g Protein: 3g Sodium: 110mg Fiber: 4g Sugar: 14g

197. Chocolate And Almond Milk Pudding

Preparation time: 10 minutes **Cooking Time:** 15 minutes **Servings:** 4 **Difficulty:** Easy
Ingredients:

- 2 cups unsweetened almond milk
- 1/4 cup cornstarch
- 1/4 cup cocoa powder
- 1/4 cup maple syrup
- 1/4 teaspoon salt
- 1 teaspoon vanilla extract
- Sliced almonds (optional topping)

Instructions:

1. In a medium saucepan, whisk together the almond milk, cornstarch, cocoa powder, maple syrup, and salt until the mixture is smooth and there are no lumps.
2. Heat the mixture over medium heat, whisking continuously until it thickens, about 10-12 minutes.
3. Remove from heat and stir in the vanilla extract.
4. Pour the pudding into 4 serving dishes and let it cool for 10-15 minutes at room temperature.
5. Cover each dish with plastic wrap and

refrigerate for at least 2 hours or until the pudding has set.

6. Serve the pudding chilled with sliced almonds on top (optional).

Nutritional Values: Calories: 124 kcal Fat: 4g Carbohydrates: 23g Fiber: 2g Protein: 2g Sodium: 166mg

198. Cherry And Almond Flour Clafoutis

Preparation time: 15 minutes **Cooking Time:** 40 minutes **Servings:** 6 **Difficulty:** Easy
Ingredients:

- 1 cup of fresh or frozen pitted cherries
- 1/2 cup almond flour
- 2 tablespoons of gluten-free all-purpose flour
- 1/4 cup of sugar
- 1/4 teaspoon of salt
- 3 large eggs
- 1 cup of lactose-free milk
- 1 teaspoon of vanilla extract
- Powdered sugar for dusting

Instructions:

1. Preheat the oven to 375°F (190°C) and grease a 9-inch (23 cm) baking dish with cooking spray.
2. Spread the pitted cherries evenly in the bottom of the dish.
3. Whisk together the almond flour, gluten-free flour, sugar, and salt in a large bowl.
4. In a separate bowl, whisk the eggs, lactose-free milk, and vanilla extract until well combined.
5. Pour the wet ingredients into the dry ingredients and whisk until the batter is smooth.
6. Pour the batter over the cherries in the baking dish.

7. Bake for 35-40 minutes, until the clafoutis is set and golden brown on top.
8. Let cool for 10 minutes before serving.
9. Dust with powdered sugar before serving.

Nutritional Values: Calories: 148 Fat: 8g Carbohydrates: 14g Fiber: 1g Protein: 6g

199. Pumpkin And Almond Flour Muffins with Cinnamon and Nutmeg

Preparation time: 15 minutes **Cooking Time:** 25 minutes **Servings:** 12 muffins **Difficulty:** Easy
Ingredients:

- 1 cup canned pumpkin puree.
- 2 eggs
- 1/2 cup maple syrup
- 1/4 cup almond milk
- 1 tsp vanilla extract
- 2 cups almond flour
- 1 tsp baking powder
- 1 tsp baking soda
- 1 tsp cinnamon
- 1/2 tsp nutmeg
- 1/4 tsp salt

Instructions:

1. Preheat the oven to 350°F (180°C). Grease a muffin tin or line it with muffin cups.
2. In a large mixing bowl, whisk the pumpkin puree, eggs, maple syrup, almond milk, and vanilla extract until well combined.
3. Whisk together the almond flour, baking powder, baking soda, cinnamon, nutmeg, and salt in a separate bowl.
4. Gradually add the dry ingredients to the

wet ingredients, whisking until the batter is smooth.

5. Spoon the batter into the prepared muffin tin, filling each cup about 3/4 of the way.

6. Bake for 25 minutes until the muffins are golden brown and a toothpick inserted into the center comes clean.

7. Allow the muffins to cool in the tin for 5 minutes, then transfer them to a wire rack to cool completely.

Nutritional Values: Calories: 158 kcal Protein: 5 g Fat: 10 g Carbohydrates: 14 g Fiber: 3 g Sugar: 8 g Sodium: 204 mg

200. Strawberry And Coconut Cream Pie with Crust

Preparation time: 30 minutes **Cooking Time:** 20 minutes (for crust) + 15 minutes (for filling) + 2 hours (for chilling) **Servings:** 8 **Difficulty:** Medium

Ingredients:

For the crust:

- 1 1/2 cups of gluten-free all-purpose flour
- 1/4 cup of coconut oil, melted.
- 1/4 cup of maple syrup
- 1/2 tsp of salt
- 1/2 tsp of cinnamon
- 3-4 tbsp of cold water

For the filling:

- 1 cup of fresh strawberries, sliced.
- 1 can of coconut cream (13.5 oz)
- 1/4 cup of maple syrup
- 1 tsp of vanilla extract
- 2 tbsp of cornstarch
- 2 tbsp of cold water

Instructions:

1. Preheat the oven to 375°F.

2. Combine the gluten-free flour, melted coconut oil, maple syrup, salt, and cinnamon in a mixing bowl. Mix well.

3. Mix 3-4 tbsp of cold water until the dough forms a ball.

4. Press the dough into a 9-inch pie pan and prick the bottom with a fork. Bake for 20 minutes or until golden brown. Set aside to cool.

5. Mix cornstarch with cold water in a small bowl and set aside.

6. Add coconut cream and maple syrup in a saucepan over medium heat. Heat until warm and the maple syrup has dissolved.

7. Add the sliced strawberries and vanilla extract to the saucepan and stir well.

8. Add the cornstarch mixture to the saucepan and whisk until the mixture thickens about 2-3 minutes.

9. Pour the filling into the cooled crust and smooth the top.

10. Chill the pie in the refrigerator for at least 2 hours or until the filling has set.

11. Serve chilled and enjoy!

Nutritional Values: Calories: 292kcal Fat: 19g Saturated Fat: 14g Carbohydrates: 30g Fiber: 2g Sugar: 11g Protein: 3g Sodium: 156mg

201. Blueberry And Almond Flour Crumble with Oats

Preparation time: 15 minutes **Cooking Time:** 30 minutes **Servings:** 6-8 **Difficulty:** Easy

Ingredients:

- 2 cups fresh blueberries
- 1/4 cup maple syrup
- 1 tbsp lemon juice
- 1/2 tsp cinnamon
- 1/4 tsp salt
- 1 cup almond flour

- 1/2 cup gluten-free rolled oats.
- 1/4 cup brown sugar
- 1/4 tsp cinnamon
- 1/4 tsp salt
- 1/4 cup melted coconut oil.

Instructions:

1. Preheat oven to 375°F (190°C).
2. Add blueberries, maple syrup, lemon juice, cinnamon, and salt in a large mixing bowl. Stir until well combined.
3. Pour blueberry mixture into an 8x8 inch baking dish.
4. Add almond flour, oats, brown sugar, cinnamon, and salt in a separate mixing bowl. Stir until well combined.
5. Pour melted coconut oil into the dry mixture and stir until the mixture becomes crumbly.
6. Sprinkle the crumbly mixture over the blueberry mixture in the baking dish.
7. Bake in the oven for 30-35 minutes or until the crumble is golden brown.
8. Allow the crumble to cool for 5 minutes before serving.

Nutritional Values: Calories: 228 kcal Fat: 15 g Carbohydrates: 23 g Fiber: 3 g Protein: 3 g

202. Chocolate And Hazelnut Spread with Gluten-Free Crackers

Preparation time: 10 minutes. **Servings:** 6
Ingredients:

- 1 cup hazelnuts
- 1/4 cup maple syrup
- 2 tbsp coconut oil
- 2 tbsp cocoa powder
- 1/4 tsp vanilla extract
- Pinch of salt
- Gluten-free crackers for serving.

Instructions:

1. Preheat the oven to 350°F (175°C) and spread the hazelnuts on a baking sheet.
2. Toast the hazelnuts in the oven for 10-12 minutes or until fragrant and golden brown.
3. Remove the hazelnuts from the oven and let them cool slightly before transferring them to a clean kitchen towel.
4. Rub the hazelnuts with the towel to remove as much of the skin as possible.
5. Add the hazelnuts to a food processor or high-speed blender and blend until a smooth nut butter forms.
6. Add the maple syrup, coconut oil, cocoa powder, vanilla extract, and salt to the hazelnut butter and blend until smooth.
7. Serve the chocolate and hazelnut spread with gluten-free crackers.

Nutritional Values: Calories: 220 Fat: 19g Carbohydrates: 13g Fiber: 3g Protein: 4g

203. Raspberry And Coconut Flour Muffins

Preparation time: 15 minutes **Cooking Time:** 20 minutes **Servings:** 12 muffins **Difficulty:** Easy
Ingredients:

- 1 cup coconut flour
- 1/2 cup almond flour
- 1 tsp baking powder
- 1/2 tsp baking soda
- 1/4 tsp salt
- 1/2 cup maple syrup
- 1/2 cup coconut oil, melted.
- 1 cup unsweetened almond milk
- 2 eggs
- 1 tsp vanilla extract
- 1 cup fresh raspberries

Instructions:

1. Preheat the oven to 350°F and line a muffin tin with paper liners.
2. Whisk together the coconut flour, almond flour, baking powder, baking soda, and salt in a large bowl.
3. Whisk together the maple syrup, melted coconut oil, almond milk, eggs, and vanilla extract in a separate bowl.
4. Add the wet and dry ingredients and stir until well combined.
5. Gently fold in the fresh raspberries.
6. Using a scoop or spoon, divide the batter evenly among the muffin cups.
7. Bake for 20-25 minutes or until a toothpick inserted in the center of a muffin comes out clean.
8. Let the muffins cool in the tin for 5 minutes, then transfer them to a wire rack to cool completely.
9. Serve and enjoy!

Nutritional Values: Calories: 184 kcal Protein: 3g Fat: 13g Carbohydrates: 14g Fiber: 6g Sugar: 6g Sodium: 121mg

204. Lemon And Almond Flour Bars

Preparation time: 15 minutes **Cooking Time:** 25-30 minutes **Servings:** 9 bars **Difficulty:** Easy

Ingredients:

- 1 cup almond flour
- 1/4 cup coconut flour
- 1/4 cup maple syrup
- 1/4 cup coconut oil, melted.
- 1 egg
- 2 tablespoons lemon juice
- 1 tablespoon lemon zest
- 1/2 teaspoon baking powder
- Pinch of salt

Instructions:

1. Preheat the oven to 350°F (180°C) and line an 8-inch (20cm) square baking dish with parchment paper.
2. Mix the almond flour, coconut flour, baking powder, and salt in a large bowl.
3. Whisk together the maple syrup, melted coconut oil, egg, lemon juice, and lemon zest in a separate bowl.
4. Pour the wet ingredients into the dry ingredients and mix until well combined.
5. Transfer the batter to the prepared baking dish and spread it out evenly.
6. Bake for 25-30 minutes or until golden brown and a toothpick inserted into the center comes out clean.
7. Let the bars cool completely in the dish before slicing them into 9 squares.
8. Serve and enjoy!

Nutritional Values: Calories: 170 kcal Fat: 13g Carbohydrates: 10g Fiber: 2g Protein: 4g

205. Mixed Berry and Almond Flour Cake with Frosting

Preparation time: 20 minutes **Cooking Time:** 30 minutes **Servings:** 8 **Difficulty:** Easy

Ingredients:

- 1 1/2 cups almond flour
- 1/4 cup coconut flour
- 1/4 cup tapioca flour
- 1 tsp baking powder
- 1/2 tsp baking soda
- 1/4 tsp salt
- 1/2 cup maple syrup
- 1/3 cup melted coconut oil.
- 3 large eggs
- 1 tsp vanilla extract

- 1 cup mixed berries (blueberries, raspberries, and strawberries)
- 1/4 cup sliced almonds.
- 1 cup gluten-free vanilla frosting

Instructions:
1. Preheat the oven to 350°F (180°C). Grease a 9-inch round cake pan with cooking spray.
2. Whisk the almond flour, coconut flour, tapioca flour, baking powder, baking soda, and salt in a mixing bowl.
3. Whisk together the maple syrup, melted coconut oil, eggs, and vanilla extract in a separate bowl.
4. Add the dry and wet ingredients and stir until well combined.
5. Fold in the mixed berries and sliced almonds.
6. Pour the batter into the prepared cake pan and smooth out the top.
7. Bake for 25-30 minutes or until a toothpick inserted in the center comes clean.
8. Let the cake cool completely in the pan on a wire rack.
9. Once cooled, remove the cake from the pan and spread the gluten-free vanilla frosting.
10. Slice and serve.

Nutritional Values: Calories: 348 kcal Fat: 25 g Carbohydrates: 26 g Fiber: 4 g Protein: 7 g Sodium: 208 mg

206. Banana And Almond Flour Pancakes with Maple Syrup

Preparation time: 10 minutes **Cooking Time:** 10 minutes **Servings:** 2 **Difficulty:** Easy
Ingredients:

- 2 ripe bananas
- 2 eggs
- 1 cup almond flour
- 1/2 tsp baking powder
- 1/2 tsp cinnamon
- Pinch of salt
- 1 tbsp coconut oil or butter for cooking
- Maple syrup for serving.

Instructions:
1. In a large mixing bowl, mash the bananas until smooth.
2. Add in the eggs and whisk until well combined.
3. Add in the almond flour, baking powder, cinnamon, and salt. Mix until everything is well combined, and there are no lumps.
4. Heat a non-stick pan over medium heat and add the coconut oil or butter.
5. Once the pan is hot, use a 1/4 cup measuring cup to scoop the batter and pour it onto the pan.
6. Cook for 2-3 minutes on each side until golden brown.
7. Repeat with the remaining batter, adding more coconut oil or butter to the pan as needed.
8. Serve the pancakes warm with maple syrup.

Nutritional Values: Calories: 377 kcal Fat: 26.6g Carbohydrates: 26.9g Fiber: 6.5g Protein: 12.6g

207. Chocolate And Coconut Flour Cake with Frosting

Preparation time: 15 minutes **Cooking Time:** 30 minutes **Servings:** 8 **Difficulty:** Easy
Ingredients:
For the cake:

- 1/2 cup coconut flour

- 1/2 cup unsweetened cocoa powder
- 1 tsp baking soda
- 1/4 tsp salt
- 4 large eggs, room temperature
- 1/2 cup maple syrup
- 1/2 cup coconut oil, melted.
- 1/2 cup unsweetened almond milk
- 1 tsp vanilla extract

For the frosting:

- 1/2 cup unsalted butter, room temperature
- 1/2 cup powdered sugar
- 1/4 cup unsweetened cocoa powder
- 1/4 cup coconut cream
- 1 tsp vanilla extract

Instructions:

1. Preheat the oven to 350°F (175°C). Grease an 8-inch cake pan with coconut oil.
2. Whisk together the coconut flour, cocoa powder, baking soda, and salt in a medium bowl.
3. In a separate large bowl, beat the eggs until fluffy. Add the maple syrup, coconut oil, almond milk, and vanilla extract and whisk to combine.
4. Slowly mix the dry and wet ingredients until fully incorporated.
5. Pour the batter into the greased cake pan and smooth the top with a spatula.
6. Bake for 25-30 minutes, or until a toothpick inserted into the center of the cake comes out clean.
7. While the cake is baking, prepare the frosting. In a medium bowl, beat the butter until creamy. Add the powdered sugar and cocoa powder and beat until smooth. Add the coconut cream and vanilla extract and continue to beat until the frosting is light and fluffy.
8. Once the cake is baking, let it cool completely in the pan.
9. Once cooled, remove the cake from the pan and frost with the prepared frosting.
10. Serve and enjoy!

Nutritional Values: Calories: 325kcal Fat: 26g Carbohydrates: 22g Fiber: 5g Sugar: 12g Protein: 5g

208. Vanilla And Almond Flour Biscotti

Preparation time: 15 minutes **Cooking Time:** 40-45 minutes **Servings:** 12 biscotti **Difficulty:** Easy

Ingredients:

- 2 cups almond flour
- 1/2 cup granulated sugar
- 1 tsp baking powder
- 1/4 tsp salt
- 2 large eggs
- 1 tbsp vanilla extract
- 1/2 cup sliced almonds.

Instructions:

1. Preheat the oven to 350°F (180°C) and line a baking sheet with parchment paper.
2. Whisk together the almond flour, granulated sugar, baking powder, and salt in a large mixing bowl.
3. In a separate mixing bowl, beat the eggs and vanilla extract until frothy.
4. Add the egg mixture to the dry ingredients and mix until well combined.
5. Fold in the sliced almonds.
6. Form the dough into a log shape about 8 inches long and 2 inches wide on the prepared baking sheet.
7. Bake for 20-25 minutes or until golden brown.

8. Remove from the oven and let cool for 10 minutes.
9. Reduce the oven temperature to 325°F (160°C).
10. Use a sharp knife to cut the log into 12 slices and place them back on the baking sheet.
11. Bake for 15-20 minutes or until the biscotti are crispy and lightly browned.
12. Allow to cool completely before serving.

Nutritional Values: Calories: 160 kcal Fat: 11 g Carbohydrates: 13 g Fiber: 2 g Protein: 5 g

209. Chocolate And Hazelnut Biscotti

Preparation time: 15 minutes **Cooking Time:** 50 minutes **Servings:** 12 **Difficulty:** Easy
Ingredients:
- 1 cup almond flour
- 1/4 cup unsweetened cocoa powder
- 1/4 cup maple syrup
- 1/4 cup melted coconut oil.
- 2 large eggs
- 1/2 tsp baking soda
- 1/4 tsp salt
- 1/4 cup hazelnuts, chopped.

Instructions:
1. Preheat oven to 350°F (175°C). Line a baking sheet with parchment paper.
2. Combine almond flour, cocoa powder, baking soda, and salt in a medium mixing bowl.
3. Whisk eggs, maple syrup, and melted coconut oil in a separate mixing bowl until well combined.
4. Add the wet and dry ingredients and stir until a sticky dough forms.
5. Fold in chopped hazelnuts.

6. Transfer the dough to the prepared baking sheet and form it into a log shape, about 12 inches long and 3 inches wide.
7. Bake for 25 minutes or until slightly firm to the touch.
8. Remove from the oven and let cool for 10-15 minutes. Reduce oven temperature to 325°F (160°C).
9. Using a serrated knife, cut the log into 12 slices.
10. Place the slices back on the baking sheet, cut side down, and bake for 20-25 minutes or until crispy and golden brown.
11. Let cool completely before serving.

Nutritional Values: Calories: 153 kcal Fat: 12.7 g Carbohydrates: 7.3 g Fiber: 2.3 g Protein: 4.3 g

210. Coconut And Almond Flour Tart with Crust

Preparation time: 20 minutes **Cooking Time:** 30 minutes **Servings:** 8 **Difficulty:** Easy
Ingredients:
For the crust:
- 1 cup almond flour
- 1/2 cup coconut flour
- 1/4 cup maple syrup
- 1/4 cup melted coconut oil.
- 1/4 tsp salt

For the filling:
- 1 can full-fat coconut milk
- 1/2 cup maple syrup
- 1/4 cup cornstarch
- 2 cups unsweetened shredded coconut
- 1 tsp vanilla extract
- 1/4 tsp salt

Instructions:
1. Preheat the oven to 350°F.

2. Combine the almond flour, coconut flour, maple syrup, melted coconut oil, and salt in a mixing bowl. Mix well to form a dough.

3. Press the dough into a 9-inch tart pan with a removable bottom. Use a fork to poke a few holes in the crust.

4. Bake the crust for 10-12 minutes or until lightly golden.

5. While the crust is baking, prepare the filling. Whisk together the coconut milk, maple syrup, and cornstarch in a medium saucepan until smooth.

6. Place the saucepan over medium heat and stir in the shredded coconut, vanilla extract, and salt.

7. Cook the mixture for 5-7 minutes, stirring frequently, until the mixture thickens, and the coconut is toasted.

8. Pour the coconut mixture into the pre-baked tart crust.

9. Bake the tart for 15-20 minutes or until the filling is set and lightly golden.

10. Remove the tart from the oven and let it cool completely before slicing and serving.

Nutritional Values: Calories: 357kcal Fat: 28g Carbohydrates: 25g Fiber: 5g Protein: 5g Sodium: 160mg

211. Strawberry And Almond Milk Sorbet

Preparation time: 10 minutes Freezing time: 4-6 hours **Servings:** 4 **Difficulty:** Easy
Ingredients:

- 2 cups of fresh or frozen strawberries
- 1 cup of almond milk
- 1/4 cup of maple syrup
- 1 tablespoon of lemon juice
- 1/4 teaspoon of vanilla extract

Instructions:

1. Wash and hull the strawberries, then place them in a blender.

2. Add the almond milk, maple syrup, lemon juice, and vanilla extract to the blender and blend until smooth.

3. Pour the mixture into a freezer-safe container and freeze for 1-2 hours.

4. After 1-2 hours, remove the container from the freezer and use a fork to scrape and mix the partially frozen sorbet.

5. Repeat step 4 every hour for 3-4 hours until the sorbet is fully frozen and has a smooth, slushy consistency.

6. Scoop the sorbet into bowls or glasses and serve immediately.

Nutritional Values: Calories: 94 kcal Fat: 2g Carbohydrates: 19g Fiber: 2g Protein: 1g Sugar: 14g

212. Blueberry And Almond Flour Donuts

Preparation time: 10 minutes **Cooking Time:** 15-20 minutes **Servings:** 6 **Difficulty:** Easy
Ingredients:

- 1 cup almond flour
- 1/4 cup tapioca starch
- 1/4 cup coconut sugar
- 1 tsp baking powder
- 1/4 tsp baking soda
- 1/4 tsp salt
- 2 eggs
- 1/4 cup almond milk
- 2 tbsp melted coconut oil
- 1 tsp vanilla extract
- 1/2 cup fresh blueberries

Instructions:

1. Preheat the oven to 350°F and grease a donut pan.

2. Whisk together almond flour, tapioca starch, coconut sugar, baking powder, baking soda, and salt in a large mixing bowl.
3. Whisk together eggs, almond milk, melted coconut oil, and vanilla extract in another bowl.
4. Add the wet ingredients to the dry ingredients and stir until just combined.
5. Fold in the fresh blueberries.
6. Spoon the batter into the greased donut pan, filling each mold about 3/4 full.
7. Bake for 15-20 minutes or until the edges are golden brown and a toothpick inserted into the center comes clean.
8. Let the donuts cool in the pan for 5 minutes, then remove them from the pan and transfer to a wire rack to cool completely.
9. Enjoy your Low FODMAP blueberry and almond flour donuts!

Nutritional Values: Calories: 199 kcal Fat: 14.5 g Carbohydrates: 14.5 g Fiber: 2.3 g Protein: 5.2 g

213. Vanilla And Coconut Milk Panna Cotta

Preparation time: 10 minutes **Cooking Time:** 10 minutes Chilling time: 4 hours or overnight **Servings:** 4 **Difficulty:** Easy
Ingredients:
- 1 can (13.5 oz) full-fat coconut milk
- 1/2 cup lactose-free whole milk
- 1/4 cup maple syrup
- 1 tsp vanilla extract
- 2 tsp unflavored gelatin
- Fresh berries or other fruit for serving.

Instructions:
1. Whisk together the coconut milk, lactose-free whole milk, maple syrup, and vanilla extract in a medium saucepan. Heat the mixture over medium heat until it starts to steam, but do not let it boil.
2. While the mixture is heating up, sprinkle the gelatin over 1/4 cup of cold water in a small bowl. Let it sit for 5 minutes until it softens and absorbs the water.
3. Once the coconut milk mixture is heated, remove it from the heat and add the softened gelatin, whisking until it is fully dissolved, and the mixture is smooth.
4. Divide the mixture evenly among 4 small ramekins or glasses. Let cool to room temperature, then cover with plastic wrap and chill in the refrigerator for at least 4 hours or overnight until the panna cotta is set.
5. To serve, run a knife around the edge of each ramekin or glass and invert it onto a plate. Top with fresh berries or other fruit as desired.

Nutritional Values: Calories: 250 Total Fat: 21g Saturated Fat: 18g Cholesterol: 0mg Sodium: 15mg Total Carbohydrate: 13g Dietary Fiber: 1g Sugars: 9g Protein: 4g

Meal Plan

Day	Breakfast	Lunch	Dinner	Dessert
1	Breakfast Muffin with Turkey	Salmon and mixed	Beef and vegetable stew	Coconut and almond flour
2	Pineapple and coconut milk	Baked sweet potato	Spaghetti squash with meat	Lemon and coconut flour
3	Breakfast burrito	Grilled salmon with roasted	Shrimp scampi	Strawberry and almond milk
4	Mixed berry smoothie	Greek yogurt chicken salad	Beef and vegetable stir-fry	Pumpkin and almond flour
5	Buckwheat porridge	Quinoa And Black Bean	Steak and vegetable stir-fry	Apple and cinnamon
6	Breakfast Salad with Mixed	Grilled shrimp skewers	Chicken and vegetable curry	Vanilla and almond flour
7	Tofu scramble with bell	Tuna and cucumber sushi	Turkey and vegetable soup	Strawberry and coconut
8	Blueberry smoothie	Egg salad with lettuce	Spaghetti with meat sauce	Chocolate and hazelnut
9	Breakfast muffins	Veggie burger with sweet	Greek yogurt chicken	Blueberry and almond flour
10	Mango and orange	Sushi roll with tuna	Beef and broccoli stir-fry	Raspberry and almond
11	Blueberry muffins	Roasted vegetable and goat	Turkey chili with avocado	Mixed berry and almond
12	Peach and almond milk	Roasted beet and goat	Balsamic glazed pork chops	Strawberry and banana
13	Spinach, banana, and almond	Shrimp and mixed	Roasted chicken with sweet	Blueberry and oatmeal
14	Chocolate and almond milk	Zucchini noodles	Steak and roasted vegetable	Chocolate and peanut
15	Breakfast Hash with Sweet	Chicken and vegetable curry	Baked eggplant Parmesan	Chocolate and hazelnut
16	Breakfast bagel with cream	Shrimp and mixed	Pork tenderloin with roasted	Coconut and almond flour
17	Breakfast wrap	Shrimp and mixed	Roasted vegetable lasagna	Mixed berry and chia seed
18	Cinnamon Rolls with Cream	Kale and quinoa salad	Baked chicken parmesan	213. Vanilla and coconut milk
19	Probiotic drink with kefir	Salmon and mixed	Vegetable and chicken curry	Pumpkin pie
20	Breakfast Bowl with Roasted	Chicken and pesto salad	Vegetable and shrimp	Chocolate and coconut
21	Breakfast quesadilla	Vegetable and tofu stir-fry	Grilled chicken with roasted	Vanilla and coconut flour
22	Breakfast Skillet with Turkey	Crab and corn chowder	Spinach and feta stuffed	Chocolate and almond milk
23	Breakfast sausage patties	Pan-seared halibut	Stuffed bell peppers	Cherry and almond flour
24	Breakfast Scones	Turkey and avocado	Stuffed chicken breasts	Chocolate and banana
25	Blueberry and an avocado	Greek salad with feta	Teriyaki salmon with brown	Banana and almond flour
26	Cherry and almond milk	Shrimp and quinoa bowl	Baked salmon with roasted	Chocolate and almond flour
27	breakfast tart with goat	Baked sea bass with cherry	Turkey meatloaf	Raspberry and coconut

28	Green smoothie with kiwi	Spinach and feta stuffed	Zucchini noodles with turkey	Blueberry and almond flour
29	Breakfast Muffin with Turkey	Garlic and herb shrimp	Baked cod with roasted	Lemon and almond flour
30	Pineapple and coconut milk	Chicken and vegetable soup	Vegetable and chicken stir-fry	Banana and almond butter

Support my Work

If you enjoyed the contents of this book and want to help me in a simple, accessible, and fast way, I'd love to hear your honest opinion. That way, other people looking for low FODMAP recipes will find my book and all my work. To do this, use the camera on your smartphone to scan the QR code or click on this link if you have the reader in the digital version.

Thank   you,   Katy.

Conclusion

Dear Reader,

We have come to the end of this cookbook dedicated to the low FODMAP diet. I hope you have drawn inspiration and helpful advice to enrich your culinary journey. Before saying goodbye, I would like to briefly recap the topics covered in these pages to refresh your memory and provide you with a final overview.

We began by exploring the low FODMAP diet and how it can be an effective tool for dealing with gastrointestinal disorders and related symptoms. Next, we looked at general symptoms that can occur at the gastrointestinal level, giving you a deeper understanding of possible causes and factors to consider in managing your digestive health.

Next, we examined the different ways to treat and manage these symptoms. Finally, we covered topics such as balanced nutrition, strategies for identifying suitable foods for your low FODMAP diet, and possible culinary alternatives for creating tasty and healthy meals.

Finally, we discussed the importance of dietary supplements and nutrients to ensure adequate nutrition during the low FODMAP journey. We explored the options available and the benefits these can provide for the well-being of your digestive system.

Now concluding this journey, I wish you the best in your future culinary adventures. The recipes and information in this cookbook have inspired you to experiment with new dishes and discover a world of delicious flavors without compromising your digestive health.

Always remember to listen to your body, care for yourself, and adapt the recipes to your needs. Be creative, explore new ingredients, and don't be afraid to test your culinary skills.

Thank you for choosing this book as your companion in your gastronomic adventures. May you enjoy optimal health, delicious dishes, and happy moments shared around the table.

Good luck and bon appétit!

Cordially, Dora Gibbons

Printed in Great Britain
by Amazon